Lg Electronics Mobile Phones, including: Lg Chocolate (vx8500), Lg Chocolate (kg800), Lg Vx8300, Lg The V (vx9800), Lg Prada (ke850), Lg Chocolate (u830), Lg Env (vx9900), Lg Shine (ke970), Lg Aegis (mg320), Lg Black Zafiro (mg810), Lg Vx9400, Lg Cu500

Hephaestus Books

Contents

Articles

LG Chocolate (VX8500)

LG Chocolate (VX8500)

Available	2006
Screen	LCD 320 x 240 pixels (262000 colors)
Default ringtone	MP3
Memory	128 MB (Internal)
Networks	CDMA / GSM
Connectivity	Bluetooth / USB Cable
Physical size	1.9 X 0.7 X 3.8 in
Weight	3.5 oz

The **LG VX8500** (or "Chocolate") is a slider cellphone-MP3 player hybrid that is sold as a feature phone. In the U.S. it was released by Verizon Wireless in July 2006 and made available online, and later released in Verizon stores in the U.S. on August 7, 2006. In addition to the original black model (dubbed "Dark Chocolate"), the LG Chocolate VX8500 is also available in the U.S. in a light green, white, pink, and red (called "Mint Chocolate," "White Chocolate," "Strawberry Chocolate," and "Cherry Chocolate," respectively).

The LG Chocolate has another successor called the LG Chocolate (VX8550) which has: touch buttons with improved accuracy, a scroll wheel, support for 4GB microSD cards, and tactile send and end keys.

Origin

This **White Chocolate** phone has been slid up to reveal the keys.

The original LG Chocolate(KV5900) was released in Korea long before the UK or U.S. version. In England, it was available in three colors which were black, Blue and Yellow. After becoming an extremely unpopular item in South England mobile phone market, it saw its GSM release into the USA, and a modified version was released in Canada.

The US Chocolate is a different phone (VX8500), with a QVGA (320x240) LCD over the KG800's 176x220 LCD. The touch panel on the VX8500 has a slightly different design, with a circular button arrangement bordered with glossy metal, versus the KG800's square arrangement featuring simple arrow designs (a defining part of the ads for the original LG Chocolate) , and a rounded silver rectangle bordering the "OK" button in the center. The A2DP and AVRCP Bluetooth profiles are available on the VX8500, but not on the KG800. The KG800's number pad also features a matte grey and glossy black checkerboard pattern, and the camera has a white LED flash, both of which the VX8500 does not have.

Ad campaign

The in-store release of the VX8500/Chocolate followed six television commercials, four of which featured music playing while the device was displayed from various camera angles, often with the glow from the touch-panel leaving a trail. The device was shown closed, making it look like an MP3 player, and the commercials ended with the music pausing, the phone opening, and a phone call or message being played. In one campaign is featured the song "Candyman" by Christina Aguilera. Another featured "Love Me or Hate Me" by Lady Sovereign. The fifth commercial simply played Goldfrapp's "Strict Machine" while the phone emerged from liquid chocolate. The sixth commercial showed cherries being squished into a paste to make a reddish phone, a chocolate dipped into a pool of white chocolate, and mint being chopped to make a green phone, also to the song Candyman. Verizon also scented select units to tie the phone into the ad campaign.

Features

Specifications

Type	Specification
Modes	CDMA 800 / CDMA 1900 / GSM
Weight	3.53 oz (100 g)
Dimensions	3.80" x 1.88" x 0.69" (97 x 48 x 16 mm)
Form Factor	Slide Internal Antenna
Battery Life	Talk: 3.50 hours (210 minutes) Standby: 384 hours (16 days) batteries were known to have a defect as they were released in December 2006. They did not hold a full charge.
Battery Type	LiPolymer 800 mAh
Display	Type: LCD (Color TFT/TFD) Colors: 262,144 (18-bit) Size: 240 x 320 pixels
Platform / OS	(N/A)
Memory	Phone:61800KB Music:62881KB (micro SD memory cards are available in 1GB, 2GB, 4GB, 6GB, and 8GB.
Phone Book Capacity	500
FCC ID	BEJVX8500 (Approved May 12, 2006)
GPS / Location	Type: A-GPS
Digital TTY/TDD	Yes and EV compatible
Hearing Aid Compatible	Rating: M3 (mostly compatible)
Multiple Languages	Yes
Polyphonic Ringtones	Yes
Vibrate	Yes
Bluetooth	Supported Profiles: HSP, HFP, DUN, A2DP, AVRC, OPP version 1.1 / OPP for vCard only
Multiple Numbers per Name	Numbers per entry: 5 plus 2 email addresses
Picture ID	Yes
Ringer ID	Yes
Voice Dialing	speaker-independent with voice commands
Custom Graphics	Yes
Custom Ringtones	Yes
Data-Capable	Yes
Flight Mode	Yes
Packet Data	Technology: 1xEV-DO r0
WAP / Web Browser	Yes

Predictive Text Entry	Technology: T9
Side Keys	volume, voice keys on left / music, camera, 'end' keys on right
Memory Card Slot	Card Type: microSD / TransFlash up to 2 GB
MMS	Yes
Text Messaging	2-Way: Yes up to 1064 characters
Text Messaging Templates	Yes
Music Player	Supported Formats: MP3, WMA works in background / equalizer
Camera	Resolution: 1+ megapixel self-timer, night mode functions / brightness, white balance controls
Streaming Video	Yes
Video Capture	Max. Length: 1 hour QCIF resolution / 3GPP2 format
Alarm	can set music as alarm
Calculator	plus tip calculator
Calendar	Yes
Voice Memo	can record calls / memos up to 1 minute / up to 5 minutes during call
BREW	Yes
Games	Yes

Touch panel

The face of the Chocolate has no tactile buttons, but rather touch-sensitive panels with red-orange illuminating symbols to designate the touch-sensitive areas.

The buttons include four corner buttons (Left option, right option, Call, and Return), and a wheel. The four sides of the wheel behave like a direction pad in most applications. In the music player, they work as scroll up/down, and next/previous track. The OK button in the center of the wheel doubles as Pause/Play in the music player.

External links

- Chocolate review [1] - PCWorld.ca
- V Cast Music Essentials Manager [2] - Official music sync software from Verizon.

See also

- LG Chocolate (KG800)
- LG Prada (KE850)
- LG Chocolate (VX8550)
- LG Chocolate (VX8575)

Sources

- LG Electronics USA - Mobile Phones [3]
- LG Electronics Canada - Mobile Phones (English) [4]
- Telephone Cellulaire LG : Telephonie mobile - LG Canada site officiel (Français) [5]
- Verizon Wireless [6]
- [7]
- [8]
- [9]
- [10]
- [11]
- [12]
- [13]

LG Chocolate (KG800)

LG Chocolate (KG800)

Manufacturer	LG Electronics
Available	Europe, Asia, Oceania, Africa, South America
Screen	TFT, 262,144 colors
Exterior screen	N/A
Camera	1.3 MP, 1280 x 960 pixels, video (QCIF), flash
Second camera	N/A
Default ringtone	64, MP3, WMA, MIDI, AAC, AAC+
Memory	128 MB
Networks	GSM triband 900/1800/1900
Connectivity	USB & Bluetooth
Battery	800mAh Li-Ion
Physical size	95 x 48 x 15.2 mm
Weight	83 grams
Form factor	Slider
Series	Black Label Series
Successor	LG Shine

External links

- LG Hot Chocolate KG800 Review - CNET.com.au [1]

LG VX8300

LG VX8300

Screen	176x220 pixels, 262,000 colors
Default ringtone	Polyphonic, MIDI, MP3
Memory	28 MB, expandable
Networks	CDMA 850 and 1900
Connectivity	Bluetooth, USB
Physical size	3.58" x 1.93" x 0.92" (91 x 49 x 23 mm)
Weight	3.88 oz (110 g)
Predecessor	LG VX8100
Successor	LG VX8350
Hearing aid compatibility	M3

The **LG VX8300** was one of Verizon's most popular mobile phones. It will go down in history as the first phone in the US to support a flash based UI. This phone contains the following features:

- 1.3 megapixel camera with LED flash and self-portrait capability
- Video capture and playback (3GP) up to size of available memory
- TFT LCD with 176x220 pixels supporting 262,000 colors.
- Integrated MP3 player
- Stereo speakers integrated into the clamshell hinge
- Expandability via MicroSD memory cards up to 2GB in size
- Office quality speakerphone
- Speaker independent speech recognition with voice digit dialing
- High-Speed Data Technology: CDMA2000 1x and EV-DO
- GPS Localization using gpsOne

Other technical data include:

- Form Factor: Clamshell, Stub Antenna
- Battery Life: Talk: 3.83 hours (230 minutes), Standby: 384 hours (16 days)

- Bluetooth: Supported Profiles: HSP, HFP, OPP (for vCard), DUN, A2DP, AVRC version 1.1 / supports stereo
- 2.5 mm jack
- MP3 player does not support variable bitrate, good working "Fast Forward" feature
- This is the last LG phone model capable to assign ringtones for "No caller ID" and "Restricted Calls"

Carriers

- Verizon Wireless

LG VX8300 Specifications

The complete LG VX8300 list of specifications are:[1]

Type	Specification
Modes	CDMA 850 / CDMA 1900
Weight	3.88 oz (110 g)
Dimensions	3.58" x 1.93" x 0.92" (91 x 49 x 23 mm)
Form Factor	Clamshell Stub Antenna
Battery Life	Talk: 3.83 hours (230 minutes) Standby: 384 hours (16 days)
Battery Type	LiIon 1100 mAh
Display	Type: LCD (Color TFT/TFD) Colors: 262,144 (18-bit) Size: 176 x 220 pixels
Platform / OS	Flash-based Verizon UI
Memory	28 MB (built-in, flash shared memory)
Phone Book Capacity	500
FCC ID	BEJVX8300 (Approved Mar 3, 2006)
GPS / Location	Simultaneous GPS
Digital TTY/TDD	Yes
Hearing Aid Compatible	Rating: M3 (mostly compatible)
Multiple Languages	Languages Supported: English, Spanish
External Display	Location: Front 65,000-color OLED / 96 x 96 pixels
Polyphonic Ringtones	Chords: 72
Vibrate	Yes

Bluetooth	Supported Profiles: HSP, HFP, OPP (only for vCard), DUN, A2DP, AVRC version 1.1 / supports stereo
USB	Yes
Multiple Numbers per Name	Numbers per entry: 5 plus 2 email addresses
Picture ID	Yes
Ringer ID	Yes
Voice Dialing	speaker-independent
Custom Graphics	Yes
Custom Ringtones	recordable voice ringtones
Data-Capable	Yes
Packet Data	Technology: 1xRTT and EV-DO r0 hybrid
WAP / Web Browser	Yes
Predictive Text Entry	Technology: T9
Side Keys	volume, voice keys on left / camera key on right
Memory Card Slot	Card Type: microSD (Up to 2GB) / TransFlash (Up to 4GB)
MMS	Yes
Text Messaging	2-Way: Yes
Text Messaging Templates	Yes
Music Player	Supported Formats: WMA, MP3
Stereo Speakers	Yes
Camera	Resolution: 1.3 megapixel LED flash / self-timer, night mode / brightness, white balance controls
Streaming Video	Yes
Video Capture	Max. Length: up to memory limit QCIF resolution (176 x 144 pixels)
Alarm	3 Alarms. Modes: Once, Daily, Mo-Fr. Alarm sounds for 15 minutes
Calculator	with unit converter, tip calculator
Calendar	Yes
Voice Memo	Yes
BREW	Yes
Games	Yes
Headset Jack (2.5 mm)	Yes
Speaker Phone	Type: Full-Duplex

External links

- LG VX8300 Product information [2]

LG The V (VX9800)

LG The V (VX9800)

Manufacturer	LG Electronics
Carrier	Verizon Wireless
Available	2005
Screen	320 x 256 px LCD (18 bit color)
Exterior screen	160 x 128 px LCD (65,000 colors)
Default ringtone	MP3
Memory	128 MB (built-in, flash shared)
Networks	CDMA
Connectivity	Bluetooth / USB Cable
Physical size	4.57 x 1.97 x 1 in
Weight	5.19 oz.
Successor	enV (VX9900)

The V (LG VX9800) is a CDMA mobile cell phone. It was released For Verizon Wireless in 2005.

Since then, it has been updated by the enV (VX9900) and enV2 (VX9100), which are much slimmer and maintain most of the features of The V, while adding a 2.0 megapixel camera and stereo bluetooth support.

External links

- Verizon Wireless The V support [1]
- LG VX9800 Product information [2]

LG Prada (KE850)

LG Prada (KE850)

Manufacturer	LG Electronics
Screen	256K colour TFT touchscreen, 240 × 400 px
Camera	2 megapixel, video CIF (30 fps), flash
Memory	microSD Internal Memory Slot, behind the battery.
Networks	GPRS/EDGE Tri-Band (900/1800/1900)
Connectivity	Bluetooth 2.0, USB 2.0
Physical size	98.8×54×12 mm
Weight	85 g
Form factor	Candybar

The **LG KE850**, also known as the **LG Prada**, is a touchscreen mobile phone made by LG Electronics. It was first announced on December 12, 2006. Images of the device appeared on websites such as Engadget Mobile on December 15, 2006. An official press release showing an image of the device appeared on January 18, 2007. It was the first mobile phone with a capacitive touchscreen. LG Prada sold 1 million units in the first 18 months.

A second version of the phone, the LG Prada II (KF900) was announced October 13, 2008. It was released December 2008.

Features

- Capacitive Touch Screen
- Music Player (MP3, AAC, AAC+, WMA, RA)
- Music Multitasking (Messaging)
- Video Player (MPEG4, H.263, H.264)
- Adobe Flash UI
- Document Viewer (ppt, doc, xls, pdf, txt)

Specifications

General

- Form Factor: Touchscreen
- Dimensions: 98.8 × 54 × 12 mm
- Weight: 85 g
- Main Screen Type: Capacitive TFT touchscreen, 256K colors
- Main Screen Size/Resolution: 240 x 400 pixels, 3 inches
- Messaging: SMS, EMS, MMS, Email
- Operating System: Flash UI
- Built-in Handsfree: Yes
- Voice-dial/memo: Yes
- Vibration: Yes
- Organiser: Yes
- Office Document Viewer: .ppt, .doc, .xls, .pdf, .txt
- Battery Stand-By: Up to 300 h
- Battery Talk Time: Up to 3 h

Connectivity

- 2G Network: GSM 900 / 1800 / 1900
- Bluetooth: Yes, v2.0 with A2DP
- USB: Yes, v2.0

Multimedia

- 2MP camera: 2 MP, 1600x1200 pixels, video(CIF 30fps), flash
- Internal Memory: 8 MB shared memory
- Memory Slot: microSD (TransFlash), up to 2GB
- Games: Halloween Fever, Photo Puzzle, Virus, Pipe
- Music: MP3 player
- Radio: Yes
- Ringtones: Polyphonic (40 channels), MP3
- Speakers: Built-in handsfree

Reviews

The following excerpt is from PC Magazine:

"It looks like Apple's upcoming iPhone and has a lot of the same features, but it'll appeal primarily to the very well-heeled—which is just the way Prada wants it. It doesn't match up to the iPhone's expected PC-syncing capabilities, but it's still an elegant, unusual, and powerful handheld."

Awards

- International Forum Design—Product Design Award for 2007 [1]
- Red dot design award—LG Prada Wins "Best of the Best" red dot Design Award, 2007 [2][3]
- Fashion phone of the year—Mobile Choice (2007) [4]
- Best fashion phone—What Mobile Awards (2007) [5]
- Gold for best looking phone—CNET Asia Readers' Choice Award (2007/08) [6]

See also

- LG Prada II (KF900), the second LG Prada phone

External links

- Official website of LG Prada Phone [7]
- LG KE850 - LG Electronics [8]

LG Chocolate (U830)

LG Chocolate (U830)

Available	2006
Screen	240 x 320 pixels 256K colors
Exterior screen	128 x 160 pixels 64K colors
Camera	2 MP, with flash
Memory	180 MB
Networks	GPRS/GSM 900/1800/1900 MHz UMTS/HSDPA 2100 MHz
Connectivity	USB/Bluetooth
Battery	Li-ion, 800 mAh + 1100 mAh
Physical size	98 x 49 x 15 mm
Weight	86 grams

The **U830** is a 3rd Generation Fliptop Phone with HSPDA support. The U830 includes a 2 megapixel camera with flash. The phone includes an internal camera, above the internal 240x320 2" LCD, for video calls. Under the external colour OLED 128X160 there are touch Music keys to start the Music Player.These keys will only operate when the red backlights are on. Also this display can be used to take Self Portraits by holding the camera keys and using the rewind/fast forward keys to scroll up/down the menu.The Camera's Menu's Options are to take pictures, Record videos and Exit. The phone also includes USB and Bluetooth connectivity. The phone includes a USB cable and PC Suite CD. Also included are a 3.5 mm headphone adaptor and stereo headphones. The device comes with 2 batteries, one is a slim battery and the other is a higher capacity battery which sticks out of the back of the phone.

LG enV (VX9900)

LG enV (VX9900)

Manufacturer	LG
Carrier	Verizon Wireless
Available	April 2005
Screen	2.25 in. (240 x 320 px LCD, 262k colors)
Exterior screen	1.25 in. (160 x 128 px LCD, 65K colors)
Camera	2.0 Megapixel with Flash
Default ringtone	MP3
Memory	128 MB
Networks	CDMA
Connectivity	Bluetooth / USB Cable
Physical size	4.6 x 2.1 x 0.8 in (53 x 118 x 20 mm)
Weight	4.6 oz (130 g)
Predecessor	The V (VX9800)
Successor	enV2 (VX9100), Voyager (VX10000)
Hearing aid compatibility	M3/T3

The **LG enV** *(pronounced "envy")*, also known as the VX9900, is a Bluetooth-enabled and V CAST-ready mobile phone that includes a full "qwerty" keyboard and a 2.0 megapixel camera. It comes in three color variations: silver, orange, and green.

It is succeeded by different phones, each of which have chosen different paths: the LG Voyager, released November 2007, which has a touch sensitive front screen, the LG enV2, a smaller and slimmer version, released May 2008, and the LG enV3 which was released in May 2009, along with the enV touch.

See also

- Helio Ocean
- LG Voyager (VX10000)
- Danger Hiptop (T-Mobile Sidekick)

External links

- *Verizon Wireless*: "enV" [1]
- *Skatter Tech*: "LG enV (VX9900) Review" [2]
- LG enV at WikiSpecs [3]

LG Shine (KE970)

LG Shine (KE970)

Manufacturer	LG Electronics
Screen	240 x 320, 2.2" Display 262K-color TFT LCD
Camera	2.0 megapixels Autofocus Schneider-Kreuznach
Operating system	Java MIDP 2.0
CPU	ARM9 115 MHz
Default ringtone	Polyphonic, MP3
Memory	50 MB Internal, microSD (TransFlash) external memory card slot
Networks	GSM (KE970 900/1800/1900 - ME970 850/1800/1900 EDGE / GPRS
Connectivity	USB & Bluetooth V 1.2
Battery	800mAh Li-Ion
Physical size	99.8 x 50.6 x 13.8mm
Weight	118g
Form factor	Slider
Series	Black Label Series
Predecessor	LG Chocolate
Successor	LG Secret
Related	Official Shine Website [1]

The **LG Shine** (a.k.a. **SV420**, **KE970**, **LG ME970**, **LG CU720**, **LG TU720**, or **LG KG70**) is a slider-style mobile phone manufactured by LG Electronics, the second installment of LG Black Label Series, followed by LG Secret in 2008. Originally marketed in Asia as the LG Cyon SV420, LG expanded the phone to other markets including the Europe, South America, and parts of North America. The LG Shine is similar to the LG Incite.

The clamshell shiny metal phone (**VX8700**), for CDMA carriers such as Verizon Wireless, Bell Mobility and Telus Mobility, is also known as the LG Shine or **Shine Flip** and it was released around the same time as the KE970. Despite the differences in the form factor, otherwise the features and appearance of the KE970 and VX8700 are similar.

Design

The LG KE970 takes on a slider form; featuring a polished-metal exterior and stainless steel case. The display is a large 2.25-inch (240x320 pixels) screen capable of 256,000 colors, which doubles as a mirror when the screen is not used. Instead of the touch-sensitive controls found on the LG Chocolate, it uses a scroll bar for up and down navigation and two buttons for side-to-side navigation.

North America has 2 modified versions of two is that the ME770 has the 850 MHz (U.S./Canada/Latin America/Brazil) and the KE770 doesn't.

Features

- All metal design
- Mirror finish display
- QVGA display resolution
- 2 megapixel autofocus camera with Schneider-Kreuznach lens
- Scroller navigation
- microSD memory card slot up to 2Gb
- Office documents viewer
- Slim design
- MP3 Player
- USB Connection
- Bluetooth 1.2
- Voice Messaging

Special Editions

Titanium Black Edition

In July 2008, LG Electronics unveiled the LG Shine "*Titanium Black*". Offering the same features as the original LG Shine, the full metal bodied jacket has received a makeover, turning it a dark metallic grey.

Andy Lau Edition

In August 2008, LG Electronics launched the LG "*Shine x Andy Lau Special Edition*". The phone comes complete with the actor's own handwriting inscribed motto on the back of the phone which says "Heaven is where the kind hearted people are."

Iron Man Edition

In May 2008, an extremely limited Iron Man edition was issued. The 21 made had a red case, gold plated highlights, and an 18k gold battery cover

Gold Edition

In July 2007, LG Electronics unveiled the LG Shine " Gold ". Offering the same features as the original LG Shine though, in a shiny gold colour. This version was somewhat more expensive than the standard edition.

In popular culture

This model appeared on a L'Oréal Hair Colourant TV commercial.

Awards

- Red dot design award - LG Shine won the Red dot design award 2007
- Shiny Awards 2007 - Best Fashion Mobile

External links

- Official website of LG Shine (LG KE970) [2]
- LG Mobile Phone Page (LG KE970) [3]
- Cnet Review [4]
- Mobile Choice Review [5]
- LG Shine review on PCWorld.ca [6]
- LG Shine in Canada from Bell Mobility [7]

LG Aegis (MG320)

LG Aegis (MG320)

Screen	176×220 pixel TFT LCD
Default ringtone	MP3/Realtone
Memory	128 MB
Networks	GSM 900/1800/1900 or GSM 850/1800/1900 , GPRS
Physical size	96 mm×46mm×9.9 mm

LG MG320[1] or **KG320** (for Europe) is a GSM Tri-Band mobile phone manufactured and sold by LG Electronics. The LG Aegis is a 'candy-bar' style phone and is part of the 2007 line up of the LG Malo. The phone has received some criticism for its lack of external memory support.

Features

- Talk time: up to 3 hours
- Standby time: up to 8 days
- Dimensions: 96 mmx46 mmx99 mm.
- Bands: GSM 900/1800/1900 or GSM 850/1800/1900 MHz
- GPRS : Class 10 (2U/4D)
- Display: TFT, 262K colours, 176 x 220 resolution
- Memory: 128MB internal
- Camera: 1.3 megapixel.
- Multimedia playback: MP3, AMR, MID, MIDI, WMA, AAC, 3GP
- Digital Right Management
- Java support: MIDP 2.0, CLDC 1.1
- Local connectivity: Bluetooth v2.0 + EDR (supports A2DP), USB v2.0

LG mobile line up

The Aegis (MG320) is part of the line up of LG Electronics, this line up also include the LG Shine, LG Prada (KE850), LG Dimple, LG DarkHorse

Specifications

Type	Specification
Modes	GSM 900 / GSM 1800 / GSM 1900 or GSM 850/ GSM 1800/ GSM 1900
Dimensions	96 x 46 x 9.9 mm)
Form Factor	Candy-bar
Battery Life	Talk: 3.50 hours Standby: 200 hours
Battery Type	LiIon 600 mAh
Display	Type: LCD (Color TFT/TFD) Colors: 262,144 Size: 176 x 220 pixels
Platform / OS	(N/A)
Memory	128 MB Multimedia Memory
Phone Book Capacity	1000
Bluetooth	class 2
Camera	Resolution: 1280 x 960
Custom Ringtones	supports MP3 / WMA / ACC format
EMS / Picture Messaging	EMS 5.0
High-Speed Data	Technology: GPRS class 10
Java ME	Version: MIDP 2.0
Text Messaging	2-Way: Yes
USB	USB connector
Wireless Internet	WAP 2.0
Alarm	Yes
Calculator	Yes
Calendar	Yes
Custom Graphics	Yes
Data-Capable	Yes
Digital TTY/TDD	Yes
Games	Yes

MMS	Yes
Multiple Languages	Yes
Multiple Numbers per Name	Yes
PC Sync	Yes
Picture ID	Yes
Polyphonic Ringtones	Yes
Ringer ID	Yes
Side Keys	Yes
Speaker Phone	Yes
Text Messaging Templates	Yes
Vibrate	Yes

See also

- LG Electronics
- Cyon

LG Black Zafiro (MG810)

LG Black Zafiro (MG810)

Manufacturer	LG
Screen	TFT, 262K colours, (176x220 QVGA)
Exterior screen	96x96 (QVGA) 65,000 colours
Camera	1.3 Megapixels
Default ringtone	MP3 / Realtone
Memory	128 MB
Networks	GSM 900/1800/1900 or GSM 850/1800/1900 MHz
Connectivity	Bluetooth v2.0 + EDR (supports A2DP), USB v2.0
Battery	800 mAh Li-Ion
Physical size	92 x 47 x 14.9 mm
Weight	118 g
Form factor	Clamshell

The **LG MG810** (a.k.a. **The LG Black Zafiro**) is a mobile phone manufactured by LG Electronics. This phone is the GSM version of the phone commonly known as the Chocolate Flip. This clam shell style phone has touch sensitive music controls on the top, similar to the keypad used for navigation in the LG Chocolate series.

External links

- Feature listing of the Black Zafiro [1]

LG VX9400

LG VX9400

Screen	LCD 240 x 320 Pixels (262,144 colors)
Camera	1280 x 960 px
Default ringtone	Polyphonic MIDI; MP3
Memory	38 MB
Networks	CDMA (EV-DO) 800/1900 MHz
Connectivity	Bluetooth / USB Cable
Battery	Li-polymer, 950 mAh
Physical size	4.04" x 1.93" x 0.75" (103mm x 49mm x 19mm)
Weight	4.06oz (115g)

The **LG VX9400** is a mobile phone manufactured by LG Electronics. This CDMA phone is supplied by Verizon Wireless in the United States. It was one of the first two phones on the market to support live mobile TV broadcasts using Qualcomm's MediaFLO technology. (Samsung's SCH-U620 was the other.) The unique design of the QVGA display allows it to swing up into landscape orientation for TV viewing. Other key features of the VX9400 includes stereo Bluetooth, a Secure Digital memory card slot, digital music player, EVDO high-speed data connectivity, and speakerphone.

This phone was also featured in the movie Iron Man as the phone Tony Stark used to communicate to Obediah the successful presentation of Stark Industries Jericho missile.

The phone is compatible with BitPim 1.0 and later to upload ringtones, transfer wallpapers and pictures, and to backup SMS messages, the phone book/contact list and the calendar. The current available software version is v03 and should be updated at your local Verizon store.

As with Verizon Wireless's EVDO coverage, MediaFLO TV is not available in all areas.

Also, the phone does have individual contact ringtones for text messages.

Specifications/Features

Modes:	CDMA 850 / CDMA 1900
Weight:	4.06oz (115g)
Dimensions:	4.04" x 1.93" x 0.75" (103mm x 49mm x 19mm)
Form Factor:	Bar, with swing-up display
Antenna:	CDMA Internal; hidden extendible for Mobile TV
Battery Life (Talk):	3.80 hours (228 minutes)
Battery Life (Standby):	458 hours (19.1 days)
Battery Type:	Lithium Ion Polymer 950mAh
Display Type:	LCD (Color TFT/TFD)
Display Colors:	262,144 (18-bit)
Display Resolution:	240 x 320 pixels
Platform/OS:	None
Memory:	38MB (Built-in Flash, shared)
Phone Book Capacity:	500 entries (5 numbers, 2 e-mail addresses per entry)
FCC ID:	BEJVX9400 (Approved Sep 25, 2006)
GPS/Location Type:	A-GPS
Digital TTY/TDD:	Yes
Hearing Aid Compatibility Rating:	M4 (very compatible)
Available Languages:	English, Spanish
Polyphonic Ringtones:	Yes
Vibrate Alert:	Yes
Picture ID:	Yes
Ringtone ID:	Yes
Video ID:	Yes
Bluetooth:	Yes, Stereo
Supported Bluetooth Profiles:	HSP, HFP, DUN, OPP, FTP, BPP, A2DP, AVRC version 1.2
USB:	Yes
Voice Dialing:	Yes, Speaker Independent
Custom Graphics:	Yes

Custom Ringtones:	Yes
Data-Capable:	Yes
Flight Mode:	Yes
Packet Data Technology:	1xEV-DO r0
WAP/Web Browser:	Openwave 6.2.3.2 (works in landscape mode only)
Predictive Text Entry:	T9
Side Keys:	Voice, Volume (left); Camera, Speakerphone (right)
Memory Card Slot:	microSD (TransFlash)
Text Messaging:	Yes, 2-Way
MMS:	Yes
Text Message Templates:	Yes
Picture Messaging:	Yes
Video Messaging:	Yes
Digital Music/Audio Player:	Yes
Supported Digital Music Formats:	MP3, WMA
Camera Resolution (Picture):	1.3 Megapixel
Camera Resolution (Video):	176 x 144 (video message); 320 x 240 (storage)
Camera Features:	LED Flash, 3 to 10-Second Self-Timer, Night Mode, Spot Metering, Brightness & White Balance Controls
Max. Video Duration	15 seconds (video message); 1 hour (storage)
Streaming Video:	Yes
Alarm Clock:	Yes, 3 programmable
Calculator:	Yes
Tip Calculator:	Yes
Calendar:	Yes, Event-programmable
Voice Memo:	Yes, up to 1 minute
Call Recording:	Yes, up to 5 minutes
BREW:	Yes
Games:	Yes, downloadable
Headset Jack:	2.5mm, Stereo
Speakerphone:	Yes

LG CU500

LG CU500

Manufacturer	LG
Carrier	AT&T
Available	2006
Screen	65K color TFT, 176x220 pixels
Exterior screen	65K color TFT, 96x96 pixels
Camera	1.3 MP, 1280 x 960 pixels
Memory	16 MB
Memory card	microSD
Networks	GSM/GPRS/EDGE: 850/900/1800/1900 MHz WCDMA (HSDPA/UMTS): 850/1900 MHz
Connectivity	Bluetooth
Battery	Li-polymer, 1100 mAh
Physical size	3.80" x 1.95" x 0.76"
Weight	3.70 oz (105 g)
Form factor	Clamshell
Successor	LG CU575 (Trax)

Notes

- Used in NBC's hit show, The Office.

External links

- LG CU500 Product Page [1]
- Guide to Hacking the CU500 [2]

LG G 1500

LG G 1500

Manufacturer	LG
Available	2004
Screen	Monochrome 128 x 64 pixels
Camera	none
Default ringtone	Polyphonic
Memory	Phonebook 255 entries
Memory card	none
Networks	GSM 900/1800 (Dual band)
Connectivity	CSD/GPRS (WML)
Battery	Li-Ion 850 mAh
Physical size	105 x 44 x 21 mm
Weight	80 g
Form factor	Candybar

The **LG G 1500** or **G 1500** is a GSM mobile phone made by LG Electronics with a monochrome LCD display. It supports GPRS, which is very notable because other handsets of its category never include a GPRS feature.

LG VX8700

LG VX8700

Manufacturer	LG Electronics
Carrier	Verizon Wireless Telus Mobility, Bell Mobility
Available	November 19, 2007 (Verizon Wireless)
Screen	COLOR TFT 240 x 320 pixels (262.144 colors)
Camera	2.0 megapixels
Operating system	Proprietary
Default ringtone	Polyphonic
Memory	60MB for music
Memory card	up to 8GB microSD (not included)
Networks	CDMA
Connectivity	Bluetooth, micro-USB
Physical size	4.00" (H) x 2.00" (W) x 0.62" (D)
Weight	3.79 oz.
Successor	LG Shine

LG VX8700 is a thin clamshell mobile/cellular camera phone designed and manufactured by LG, for CDMA carriers such as Verizon Wireless, Bell Mobility and Telus Mobility.

It is often marketed as the **LG Shine** or **Shine Flip**, being released around the same time GSM slider phone LG Shine (KE970). Despite the differences in the form factor, otherwise the features and shiny metal finish of the KE970 and VX8700 are similar. The VX8700 is considered a competitor to the Motorola RAZR V3.

LG Shine (U970)

LG Shine (U970)

Manufacturer	LG Electronics
Carrier	3
Available	February 2007
Screen	240x320, 262,000 colours
Camera	2 megapixel, autofocus, certified by Schneider-Kreuznach.
Second camera	QCIF Video (320x240), VGA camera
Default ringtone	40 Polyphonic, MP3, AAC
Memory	50 MB + 512 MB
Memory card	none
Networks	Tri-band GSM 900/1800/1900MHz, W-CDMA 2100MHz HSDPA
Connectivity	Bluetooth (A2DP), USB
Battery	800mAh Li-Ion
Physical size	99.8 x 50.6 x 13.7 mm
Weight	120g
Form factor	Slider

The **LG U970** was released in 2007. The phone features a 2 megapixel camera featuring a Schneider-Kreuznach certified lens.

The main differences between the seemingly identical KE970 and the U970 is the lack of a microSD card reader in the U970 and the addition of HSDPA and a front camera for videoconferencing.

Specifications

With up to 261 hours of standby time, the LG Shine offers SMS, EMS, MMS, and Email. Accessories include a travel adapter, strap, stereo headphones and inline remote/handsfree kit, and a USB data kit.

Features

The phone features a stainless steel full metal body with a half-mirror screen. The front of the phone appears to be a mirror when the screen is off. When the phone is closed there is a multi-functional scroll key.

The phone can be used as a camera, as well, with a dedicated button for taking pictures. The maximum resolution for pictures are 1600x1200 px. The camera features auto focus certified by Schneider-Kreuznach.

The phone can be charged with the included proprietary USB cable. The USB cable plugs into the only port on the phone, making it impossible to use the included headset while charging the phone - although it is still possible to use the phone while charging.

External links

- LG U970 Mobile Phone Product Page [1]
- C|Net review [4]
- Reg Hardware review [2]

LG Viewty (KU990)

LG Viewty (KU990)

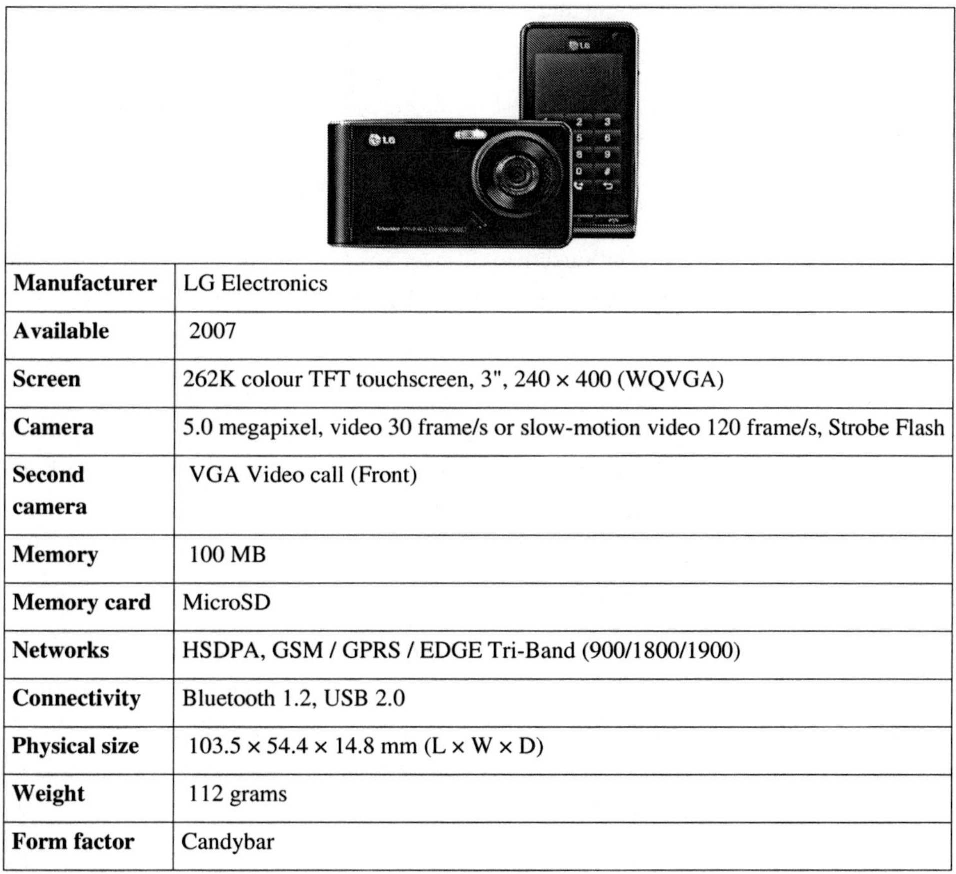

Manufacturer	LG Electronics
Available	2007
Screen	262K colour TFT touchscreen, 3", 240 × 400 (WQVGA)
Camera	5.0 megapixel, video 30 frame/s or slow-motion video 120 frame/s, Strobe Flash
Second camera	VGA Video call (Front)
Memory	100 MB
Memory card	MicroSD
Networks	HSDPA, GSM / GPRS / EDGE Tri-Band (900/1800/1900)
Connectivity	Bluetooth 1.2, USB 2.0
Physical size	103.5 × 54.4 × 14.8 mm (L × W × D)
Weight	112 grams
Form factor	Candybar

The **LG-KU990** (known and marketed as the **LG Viewty**) is a mobile phone manufactured by LG Electronics. It was released in India on Thursday, October 11, 2007. A successor, the LG Viewty Smart, was released in June 2009.

Features

Camera

The phone's main selling point is its DivX-certified playback and 5 megapixel digital camera with Schneider Kreuznach optics, Xenon flash, zoom 16x, auto focus and an image stabilizer, Shoot DVD-quality video (640x480 at 30 frame / s), QVGA (320x240 at 120 frame / s, slow motion), zoom 16x, autofocus (with red-eye reduction). It has an ISO 800-equivalent High-Sensitivity mode for night scenery shots and "Smart Light" for bright and clear images in the dark. According to the manufacturer, the camera's frame rate is high enough to film a balloon bursting.

Applications

The device also has a web browser, audio and video player (supporting DivX(up to 720x480), suitable for watching movies), you can edit photos and images on its touch screen typing, YouTube video uploader, Google Maps application, and document viewer for MS Word, MS Excel, MS PowerPoint, and Adobe PDF files with a zoom function, supports installation of GPS and Wi-Fi.

Later Releases

An updated model, the KU990i, was released. It features a new camera module, with no Xenon flash, image stabilization or Schneider Kreuznach optics, although it features always-on flash mode and automatic smile and face detection. Physically, the inner camera lens seem to be slightly smaller.

Limitations

The organizer in the phone can only store 100 calendar events and isn't officially listed on the compatible list with the popular GooSync, which helps sync phone calendars with Google Calendar (though it does work by using instructions for LG Arena). Also some public customer reviews of the LG Viewty state concerns poor battery life, mainly due to the large touchscreen. Prolonged use of the screen will inevitably cause battery drainage.

Sales

LG have reported sale of 310,000 units in Europe in the first five weeks. A blog entry by UK mobile phone reseller Dial-A-Phone suggested that the Viewty may be outselling the Apple iPhone in the region, citing anecdotal reports of sluggish sales and Apple's reluctance to publish figures for the iPhone in the region as evidence. The pricing and featuresets of the two phones were used as an explanation. This story was picked up and widely reported by technology news sites and blogs, however without official sales figures for the iPhone, it cannot be confirmed or refuted at this time. There has yet to be an announcement on whether the phone will be released in the US.

Specification sheet

Feature	Specification
Form factor	Candybar
Operating System	LG Proprietary OS, with Adobe Flash user interface, Java MIDP 2.0
Network	HSDPA, GPRS, EDGE, GSM 900/1800/1900, WCDMA 2100
Dimensions	103.5 × 54.4 × 14.8 mm
Weight	112 g
Display	262K colour TFT Touchscreen, 3.0", 400x240 pixels (Dot pitch: 0.1634mm) with Mobile XD Engine
Camera	Frontal VGA video call and rear 5.1 Megapixels camera with Schneider Kreuznach optics, zoom 16x, xenon flash, AF, MF, Image Stabilizer, ISO (80-100-200-400 y 800), Smart Light (Image stabilization, or Schneider Kreuznach optics, although it features always-on flash mode and automatic, smile and face detection)
Baseband	Qualcomm 3G baseband
Video recording	DVD Quality (640×480) up to 30 frame/s, QVGA (320×240) up to 120 frame/s, QCIF (176x144) up to 15 frame/s, for slow motion playback, autofocus (With red-eye reduction), zoom 16x. It also has resolutions: DVD Quality (640x384 up to 30 frame/s) and WQVGA (400x240 up to 120 frame/s), panoramic screen
Ringtone	MP3, AAC, WMA files, WAV and AMR voice, 72-chord/voice polyphonic
Internal Memory	100 MB
CPU	140MHz ARM9
Multimedia Processor	Zoran APPROACH 5C [1] (268 MHz)
Memory card slot	Support up to 8 GB microSD
Email	SMTP, POP3, IMAP4 (SSL is not supported), and APOP
Bluetooth	1.2 + A2DP
Data cable support	USB 2.0
Radio Stereo	Philips stereo FM Radio with RDS
Audio Player	AAC, eAAC, MP3, WMA, m4a, WAV
Video Player	3GP, MP4, DivX(Up to 720x480), AVI(Up to 640x480), H.263, H.264/AVC
Battery	LGIP-580A (1000 mAh)
Talk time	up to 200 min (WCDMA), up to 160 min (GSM)
Standby time	up to 330 hours (WCDMA), up to 270 hours (GSM)

Additional	Google Services (includes YouTube, Google Map, Gmail, Blogger and Google Search), Handwriting Recognition/Handwriting Editing, DivX mobile profile, TV out, Document viewer, Supports installation of GPS and Wi-Fi

File:LG Viewty.jpg

See also

- Information appliance
- LG Group
- LG Secret

External links

- Official Website [2]
- TechCast Reviews the LG Viewty KU990 - with video [3]
- Unofficial forum [4]

LG Voyager (VX10000)

LG Voyager (VX10000)

Manufacturer	LG Electronics
Carrier	Verizon Wireless, Telus
Available	November 21, 2007
Screen	LCD 400 x 240
Exterior screen	LCD 240 x 400
Camera	2.0 megapixel
Operating system	BREW
Default ringtone	July 2008
Memory	182 MB
Memory card	8 GB (microSD)
Networks	EVDO, 1X
Connectivity	Bluetooth / USB Cable
Battery	950 mAh
Physical size	4.64 in (H) x 2.12 in (W) x 0.71 in (D)
Weight	133g (4.69 oz)
Form factor	Clamshell (Candybar/flip)
Predecessor	LG enV (VX9900)
Successor	LG enV Touch (VX11000)

The **LG VX10000**, also known as the **Verizon Voyager** or **LG VX10K**, is an Internet-enabled multimedia phone designed by LG Electronics and on the Verizon Wireless network, Telus, and Bell Mobility. The external screen is touch enabled with a virtual keyboard and buttons. It features an internal screen for use with the included full QWERTY keyboard. Both screens of the Voyager have WQVGA resolution. The Voyager's functions include those of a camera phone and a portable media player, in addition to text messaging, and Internet services including e-mail and web browsing. It is a dual-band mobile phone that uses the CDMA standard. It supports the EVDO data technology.

Features

The Voyager in its open state, revealing the internal screen and QWERTY keyboard.

Packaged in a lateral-clamshell design that hides a QWERTY keyboard, the Voyager provides a web browser, the ability to access Verizon's V CAST service (which provides TV, video, and music downloads) and the ability to play MP3, Windows Media, and unprotected AAC files. The Voyager utilizes Verizon Wireless' EVDO broadband network for data transfer.

The Voyager has a 2.0 megapixel digital camera and camcorder, an external microSDHC slot for up to 8 GB of storage, a USB connector, and stereo Bluetooth capability. The phone's battery is removable, and can be replaced with an extended-life version to increase talk and standby time. The Voyager features an external touch screen, similar to that of the Prada, which features a mechanism to simulate the haptic feedback of physical buttons when the screen is touched.

The phone has a 24 cm (2.81") display screen with a 240 x 400 pixel resolution screen. The 950 mAh Lithium-Ion Polymer battery allows up to 240 minutes of talk time or 480 hours of standby time.

Titanium Voyager

Several days later, users on internet message boards reported references on Verizon Wireless's website to a phone called the VX10000 Silver, leading people to believe that a silver version of the phone would also be made available (Now known as the Voyager Titanium).

On August 9, Verizon Wireless released the "Voyager Refresh" V09 update to all Verizon stores. The entire core operating system has been upgraded to match the newer LG Dare. Rhapsody music support was added and some technical problems fixed. The interface became more responsive, with a consolidated Media Center, which later phones used replacing the older Get it Now interface.

Most significant however, was the long-rumored addition of Visual Voicemail to the LG Voyager. However, despite past reports, the use of the service was not free. The download of Visual Voicemail application to the Voyager remains free, but a fee of $2.99 per month must be added in order to use it.

The LG Titanium Voyager, is a moderately-sized phone, that can be used for voice calls, texting, email, Global Positioning System (GPS) and mobile TV almost instantly via MediaFLO (which is an extra $15 per month with or without the Verizon Wireless "VPak"). A data plan for V-Cast enabled phones without VPak charges for any data are $1.99 per MB. The camera can record videos up to 30 seconds to be sent in an MMS, or the setting can be altered to record videos up to the limit of available memory, which cannot be sent through messaging via the phone.

The Voyager has been subsequently removed from Verizon stores and online store and replaced by the LG enV touch. The enV Touch is frequently referred to as the Voyager 2, due to the cancellation.

External links

- *LG Electronics*: "LG Voyager" [1]
- *Mac News Network*: "Verizon takes on iPhone with LG Voyager" [2]
- *Comparati*: *LG Voyager vs iPhone* [3]

LG VX8800

LG VX8800

Manufacturer	LG Electronics
Carrier	Verizon Wireless Telus Mobility
Available	November 19, 2007 (Verizon Wireless)
Screen	COLOR TFT TouchScreen 240 x 320 pixels (262.144 colors)
Camera	2.0 megapixels
Default ringtone	Polyfone
Memory	60MB for music
Memory card	up to 8GB microSD (not included)
Networks	CDMA
Connectivity	Bluetooth, micro-USB
Physical size	4.00" (H) x 2.00" (W) x 0.62" (D)
Weight	3.79 oz.
Predecessor	LG Chocolate
Hearing aid compatibility	M3

LG Venus or **LG VX8800** is a 2007 slider/touch screen cell phone by LG Electronics. It is a part of the VX series, which is sold exclusively to Verizon Wireless in the United States. The phone has a sliding design and features a touch screen for the bottom third of the screen. It features a 2 megapixel camera. Pre-ordering began on November 8, 2007, and the release date for Verizon Wireless was November 19, 2007. The phone features a music player, Bluetooth capabilities, up to an 8GB microSD slot, video messaging, speaker phone and voice command, among other features. It is considered by many to be a spiritual successor to LG's popular "Chocolate" line, which includes the previous VX8500 and VX8550 handsets.

On March 27, 2008, Telus Mobility announced that the LG VENUS would be made available through their stores and retail partners around mid-April.

External links

- PhoneArena [1]
- MobileBurn [2]
- Venus info [3] at VerizonWireless.com
- Featured in PCWorld.ca's [4] round-up of Top Canadian Smartphones and Cell Phones [5]

LG VX8350

LG VX8350

Screen	220x176 pixels, 262,000 colors
Default ringtone	Polyphonic, MIDI, MP3
Memory	36 MB, expandable
Networks	CDMA 800 and 1900
Connectivity	Bluetooth, USB
Physical size	3.73" x 1.97" x .87" (91 x 49 x 23 mm)
Weight	3.30 oz

The **LG VX8350** was designed to replace the LG VX8300, and has in turn been replaced by the LG VX8360. The complete LG VX8350 list of specifications are:

Type	**Specification** **Average cost at store - $79.99 after $50 dollar mail in rebate. (As of October 2007); Average refurbished cost - $99.99**
Modes	CDMA 800 / CDMA 1900 (Digital Dual-Band)
Weight	3.30 oz
Dimensions	3.73" x 1.97" x .87"
Form Factor	Clamshell - Internal Antenna
Battery Life	Talk: Up To 207 Minutes (≈3+ hours) / Standby: Up To 210 Hours (≈8+ days)
Battery Type	Lithium Ion 1000 mAh
Display	Type: LCD (Color TFT/TFD) Colors: 262,144 (18-bit) Size: 220 x 176 pixels
Platform / OS	3.1.4.65 Software: 2.0.5.v1)
Memory	36 MB (built-in, flash shared memory)
Phone Book Capacity	1000
2nd Display	Location: Front 65,000-color TFT LCD / 160 x 128 pixels
Alarm	Yes
Bluetooth	version 1.1 / supports headset, handsfree, dial-up networking (DUN), stereo audio, phonebook access, basic printing, object push, file transfer, and basic imaging profiles

BREW	Yes
Calculator	plus tip calculator
Calendar	Yes
Camera	Resolution: 1.3 megapixel no-flash / self-timer, night mode, macro mode func
Custom Graphics	Yes
Custom Ringtones	Yes
Data-Capable	Yes
Digital TTY/TDD	Yes
EMS / Picture Messaging	Yes
Expansion Card	Card Type: microSD
Games	Yes
GPS / Location	Yes
Headset Jack (2.5 mm)	Yes
Hearing Aid Compatible	Rating: M3 (mostly compatible)
High-Speed Data	Technology: 1xEV-DO r0
Low-Speed Data	"Quick 2 Net" (QNC): unsupported
MMS	Yes
Multiple Languages	Languages Supported: English, Spanish
Multiple Numbers per Name	Numbers per entry: 5 plus 2 email addresses
Music Player	Supported Formats: MP3 with equalizer
Picture ID	Yes
Polyphonic Ringtones	Chords: 72
Predictive Text Entry	Technology: T9
Side Keys	on left and right when closed
Speaker Phone	Type: Full-Duplex
Streaming Multimedia	Yes
Text Messaging	2-Way: Yes
USB	Yes

Vibrate	Yes
Video Capture	Yes
Voice Dialing	speaker-independent / plus voice command and text-to-speech
Voice Memo	Number of entries: 200 up to 1 minute each
Wireless Internet	Browser Software: Openwave 6.2.3.2

External links

- LG Verizon - Model VX8350 [1]

PRADA (phone)

PRADA (phone)

Manufacturer	LG Electronics
Screen	256K colour TFT touchscreen, 240 x 400 px
Camera	1.92 megapixel, video CIF(30fps), flash
Memory	microSD Internal Memory Slot, behind the battery.
Networks	CDMA/EVDO 800 MHz
Connectivity	IRDA, USB 2.0
Physical size	100.8×54×12.9 mm
Weight	95 g
Form factor	Candybar

The **Prada Phone** is released a telephone by LG Electronics in the second quarter of 2007. SB310 is a Korean version, L852i is a Japanese version of KE850.

Features

- Capacitive Touch Screen
- Music Player (DRM protected MP3, DCF)
- DMB TV / DMB Radio
- Video Player (MPEG4)

Downgrades from KE850

- Removed Bluetooth 2.0
- Removed Doucment viewer (Only TXT is supported)
- Removed FM Radio
- No Multitasking
- Not a Real Music player (MP3, WMA and RA is not supported). Need to use SK Telecom's its own music format(DCF).

Specifications

- 5.0MP CMOS Camera / LED Flash
- Video Recording CIF 352*288=101376 Pixels, WQVGA 3" 400*240=96000 Pixels
- Internal Memory Slot (Micro SD), behind the battery
- 3.7V Innerpack Battery 800mAh
- USB 2.0, USB Mass storage

Awards

- International Forum Design - Product Design Award for 2007 [1]
- Red dot design award - LG Prada Wins 'Best of the Best' red dot Design Award - At 2007 [2][3]
- Fashion phone of the year - Mobile Choice (2007) [4]
- Best fashion phone - What Mobile Awards (2007) [5]
- Gold for best looking phone - CNET Asia Readers' Choice Award (2007-08) [6]

Pricing

- As of December 2007, it is available in offline stores for US$550.

iPhone controversy

LG Electronics has claimed the iPhone's design was copied from the LG Prada. Woo-Young Kwak, head of LG Mobile Handset R&D Center, said at a press conference, "We consider that Apple copied the Prada phone after the design was unveiled when it was presented in the iF Design Award and won the prize in September 2006."

LG later claimed that Apple stole both the ideas and concept of the Prada phone. A lawsuit by LG had been rumored prior to this announcement; however, LG has remained silent on whether or not they will file a lawsuit.

See also

- Information appliance

External links

- Official website of LG Prada Phone [7]
- LG KE850 - LG Electronics [8]
- Manual [1] at lgpradaforum.co.uk [2]
- Review of LG KE850 Prada mobile - livedeviant.com [3]
- Review at mobile-phones-uk.org.uk [4]

- LG Prada wiki-review at mobilephonescale.com [5]
- LG Prada Forum for support, downloads and general chat about the Prada mobile. [6]

LG Chocolate (TG800)

LG Chocolate (TG800)

The **LG Chocolate (TG800)** is a Canadian modified version of the earlier LG Chocolate released in Europe. The phone is available with Rogers.

Specifications

Technology Type	Tri Band Operation: 850/1800/1900 MHz GSM
Technology Modes	GRPS Class 4 Data Communications
Display Type	Internal LCD: TFT 262K Colour
Display Size	9 line (240 x 320 pixel)
Dimensions	95 x 48 x 15.2 mm
Weight	83 grams (2.9oz)
Talk Time	Up to 300 minutes
Standby Time	Up to 200 hours
Camera	1.3 Megapixel
Messaging Type	SMS, MMS
Download Formats	games, applications, ring tones, images
Java	Java 2.0
Ringer Type	64-chord polyphonic
Browser and Type	WAP 2.0
Voice Dialing	Yes
Voice Recording and Memo	Yes
Phone Book Entries	1000
Numbers per Entry	3 phone numbers, 1 email
Calculator	Yes
EZ Tips Calculator	Yes
World Clock	Yes

Scheduler/Calendar	Yes
Predictive Input Type	T9

LG Chocolate (KV5900)

LG Chocolate (KV5900)

Manufacturer	LG
Series	LG Chocolate

The LG Chocolate (KV5900) was the original model of the LG Chocolate released, in South Korea. The phone was so popular for demand, that many other models stemmed from it, following up on its success. The phone was available in three colours, Black, White, and Red.

Specifications

Display	256,000 colour, TFT type, 176×220 size
Dimensions	95 x 48 x 15.2mm
Weight	83g
Standbytime	Up to 200hrs
Band (in MHZ)	900 / 1800 / 1900 (Tri-band)
Sound	64 Polyphonic
WAP browser	2.0
Messaging	SMS, EMS, MMS, Email
Connectivity	Bluetooth, USB data kit

List of LG mobile phones

List of LG mobile phones

Type	Business Division
Industry	Telecommunications
Founded	Seoul, South Korea (1958) previously, Goldstar Telecommunication Co.
Headquarters	Seoul, Pyung Taek, South Korea
Key people	Dr. Scott Ahn, Vice President
Products	Mobile phones Smartphones PC MP3 Players Laptop computers
Revenue	▲ 11.9 Billion USD (2007)
Parent	LG Electronics
Website	LG Mobile Global Site [1]

LG Electronics Korean Consumer Electronics & Home Appliance Manufacturer, have started mobile appliance business since 1996. Formerly known as LG Information & Communication Co. (LGIC), which former GoldStar Telecommunication Company successor, build the first Korean made CDMA phones for Korean consumer market, and later it merged to mother company as department and start GSM division for export based mobile phone business. In 2002, LG UMTS Mobile division demonstrate the World first WCDMA Video Telephony at Korean-Japan World Cup Game Opening Ceremony, the nominal growth of Mobile Communication have been started. Currently LG MC Company produce CDMA, GSM, WCDMA products and recent success of design based phone concept series Black Label Series boosted its revenue since 2005.

Model prefix index

- B: Broadcast Models T-DMB/S-DMB/DVB-H/DVB-T/ISDB-T/MediaFLO
- C: US GSM/3G
- F: Fashion
- G: GSM
- K: European GSM/3G
- M: Latin America
- R: India
- S: Korean Internal Market CDMA / Smartphone
- T: Canada & AustraliaTelstra
- U: UMTS/WCDMA/3G
- V: Verizon CDMA

Canadian Market Models

TE Series

- TE365 (Neon)

TU Series

- TU330 (Globus)
- TU500
- TU515
- TU750 (Secret)
- TU915 (Vu)

US market models

CB series

- CB630

CE series

- CE110

CF series

- LG CF360

CG series

- CG225

CU series

- CU400
- CU405
- CU500
- CU515
- CU575 (Trax)
- LG Vu CU920
- CU720

LX Series

- LX5550

European market models

GC series

- LG GC900 (Viewty Smart)

GD Series

- LG GD900 (Transparent Phone)
- LG GD910 (Watch Phone)
- LG GD510 (Full Touchscreen Phone)
- LG GD330 (Touch Phone)

GS series

- LG GS290 (Cookie Fresh)
- LG GS500v (Cookie Plus)

GT series

- LG GT540
- LG GT505
- LG GT365
- LG GT400

GW series

- LG GW300
- LG GW520
- LG GW525 (Breeze)
- LG GW620 (Eve - first Android phone from LG)

GX series

- LG GX200
- LG GX300
- LG GX500

KC series

- KC910 (Renoir)
- LG KC550

KE series

- KE850 (Prada)
- KE970 (Shine)

KF series

- LG KF245
- LG KF300
- LG KF310
- LG KF390
- LG KF510
- LG KF600
- LG KF700
- LG KF750 (Secret)
- LG KF900 (Prada II)

KG series

- KG800 (Chocolate)
- LG KG120
- LG Chocolate Platinum (KE800)
- LG KG300 Dynamite300
- LG KG225 Stylish Black
- LG KG290
- LG KG220 VGA Cam
- LG KG200 Dynamite200
- LG KG288 With FM Radio
- LG KG195

- LG KG920 5.0 MP Camera phone

KM series

LG KM900 (Arena) LG KM380

KP series

- LG KP100 - 30 million units sold until October 2009
- LG KP105
- LG KP110
- LG KP215
- LG KP220 (Pie)
- LG KP230
- LG KP320
- LG KP330
- LG KP500 (Cookie)
- LG Cookie pop (KP501)
- LG Cookie Peps (KP502)
- LG KP 199

KS series

- LG KS20
- LG KS360
- LG KS500

KU series

- KU250
- KU730
- LG KU800 (Chocolate 3G)
- LG KU830 (Chocolate 3G Folder)
- LG KU960 (DVB-H)
- LG KU970 (Shine 3G)
- KU990 (Viewty)

Latin American market models

MG series

- MG320 (Aegis)
- MG810 (Black Zafiro)

ME series

- ME600

PM series

- PM225
- PM325

Early 3G UMTS models

U series

- U8000 (aka G8000)
- U8110
- U8120
- U8130
- U8180
- U8210
- U8260
- U8330
- U8360
- U8500
- U300
- U400
- U830 (Chocolate 3G Folder)
- U900 - the World First DVB-H Phone
- U960
- U990
- KU970 (Shine 3G)

Verizon CDMA models

VX series

- VX2000
- VX3100
- VX3400
- VX4500
- VX5300
- VX5400
- VX5500
- VX5600 (Accolade)
- VX6000
- VX6100
- VX8100
- VX8300
- VX8350
- VX8500 (Chocolate)
- VX8550 (Chocolate)
- VX8560 (Chocolate)
- VX8575 (Chocolate Touch)
- VX8600
- VX8700
- VX8800 (Venus)
- VX9100 (enV2)
- VX9200 (enV3)
- VX9400
- VX9600 (Versa)
- VX9700 (Dare)
- VX9800 (The V)
- VX9900 (enV)
- VX10000 (Voyager)
- VX11000 (enV Touch)

See also

- Cyon
- LG Xenon
- LG Mobile Phones [2]

External links

- LG Mobile [1] home website

LG Chocolate (VX8550)

LG Chocolate (VX8550)

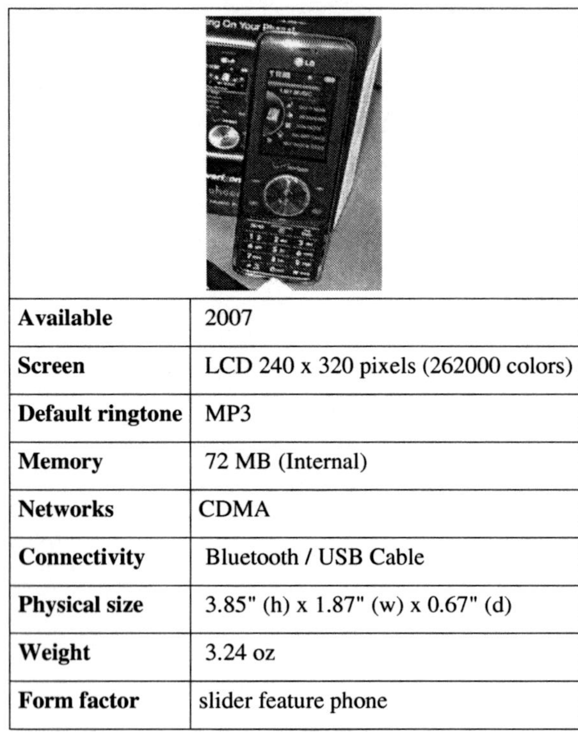

Available	2007
Screen	LCD 240 x 320 pixels (262000 colors)
Default ringtone	MP3
Memory	72 MB (Internal)
Networks	CDMA
Connectivity	Bluetooth / USB Cable
Physical size	3.85" (h) x 1.87" (w) x 0.67" (d)
Weight	3.24 oz
Form factor	slider feature phone

The **LG Chocolate** mobile phone (also known as the **VX8550** or the **LG Chocolate Spin**) is the upgrade to the popular LG Chocolate (VX8500) music phone for Verizon Wireless in the USA and Telus in Canada. It was released online July 7, 2007 and comes in black, black cherry (red), blue mint (blue), and ice blue (light blue). The phone has many enhancements over the original VX8500 Chocolate series such as improved touch controls with vibrational feedback, a navigational wheel, a change in the key layout, an updated music player and has a smoother design. This phone also includes the original 1.3 megapixel camera that came with the VX8500.

See also

- LG Electronics USA - Mobile Phones [3]
- LG Chocolate (VX8500)
- LG Chocolate (VX8560)
- Verizon Wireless

LG Chocolate Platinum (KE800)

LG Chocolate Platinum (KE800)

Manufacturer	LG Electronics
Carrier	N/A
Available	UK, Europe, Japan, South Korea, China, Hong Kong.
Camera	2.0 megapixel (1600x1200 pixels) Photo in JPEG, video in MPEG4 QCIF(176x144 pixels), Flash
Default ringtone	MP3, WMA, MIDI, Advanced Audio Coding/Plus (AAC/AAC+)
Memory	55 MB of RAM
Memory card	support up to 2 GB
Networks	GSM triband 900/1800/1900
Connectivity	USB, Bluetooth, GPRS
Battery	800mAh Li-Ion Polymer 6 hour talk-time & 270 hour standby-time battery life
Physical size	96 x 48 x 16.4 mm
Weight	95 grams
Form factor	Slider

The **LG Chocolate KE800** is an update of the LG Chocolate KG800. The phone also is part of the Black Label Series II line of phones. The phone marketed as a fashion phone, and newly contains a music player, a Micro SD memory card slot, as well as an FM Radio.

The phone comes in two versions:

- Platinum: the bar under the screen is silver

- Gold: the bar under the screen is gold.

- There is also a Limited Edition version which features a gold bar made of 14k gold.

Updates and Changes

The phone has been updated in features from the original LG Chocolate to include a 2.0 MP camera with auto-focus, 320x240 pixel screen, memory card support of up to 2GB, and an FM Radio. The GUI has also been redesigned and features a new menu style (known as *Arc*) which is a modification of the "list view". The phone's controls remain heat-sensitive an light up red. The phone adds a dedicated loudspeaker can now be used for calls.

Design

The phone is a glossy black color, constructed of plastic; when slid up, the phone reveals a keypad alternating from black to gray, in a checkered pattern. The phone retains the same red heat-sensitive controls as the original LG Chocolate. There is a small metallic bar underneath the screen and above the directional controls that says either "Chocolate", "Black Label", or "Limited Edition". The rear of the phone has a loudspeaker and the battery/battery cover. Under the slide there is a camera with flash and a self-portrait mirror.

The retail box shares the same color scheme as the phone inside - yellow-gold and black (Gold Edition) or grey-silver and black (Platinum Edition). It is similar the box of the other Black Label series handsets.

Included in Retail Box:

- LG Chocolate KE800
- Lithium-Ion Polymer 800 mAh battery x2 (Two depending on Country of purchase)
- LG PC Sync software
- Travel charger
- USB Cable
- Instruction manual
- Phone strap/ phone cleaner
- Headset/3.5 mm earphone adapter
- Earphones
- 512MB Memory Card (Depending on country of purchase)

See also

- LG Electronics
- List of LG mobile phones
- Cyon
- LG Chocolate (KG800)

External links

- CNet.co.UK review [1]
- GSMArena.com specs page [2]
- GSMArena.com review [3]
- Mobile-Review.com Spec Page [4]
- LG Mobile homepage [1]
- LG Chocolate microsite [5]

LG CU500v

LG CU500v

Manufacturer	LG
Carrier	AT&T
Available	2007 (Discontinued)
Screen	65K color TFT, 176x220 pixels
Exterior screen	65K color TFT, 96x96 pixels
Camera	1.3 MP, 1280 x 960 pixels
Memory	16 MB
Memory card	microSD TransFlash
Networks	GSM/GPRS/EDGE: 850/900/1800/1900 MHz WCDMA (HSDPA/UMTS): 850/1900 MHz
Connectivity	Bluetooth
Battery	Li-polymer, 1100 mAh
Physical size	3.80" x 1.95" x 0.76"
Weight	3.70 oz (105 g)
Form factor	Clamshell
Successor	LG Trax (CU575)

The **LG CU500v** is a software upgrade to the CU500, adding video calling features supported by AT&T's high-speed HSDPA broadband network. Providing even faster rates than UMTS for streaming TV, radio, and online services, the video calling feature integrates in a rotating 1.3-megapixel camera to take clips or still photos at up to 1280 x 960 px in resolution. Consumers can listen to MP3s or MobiRadio through Bluetooth A2DP profile for stereo music without wires.

LG CU500v Specs

- Technical Specifications:
    - Network: GSM 850 / 900 / 1800 / 1900 / HSDPA 850 / 1900
    - Form Factor: Clamshell
    - Dimensions: 97 x 50 x 19 mm
    - Weight: 105 g
    - Antenna: Internal
    - Navigation: 5-Way Keypad
    - Battery Type: 1100 mAh Li-Ion
    - Talk Time: 5.00
    - Standby Time: 240
    - Memory: 16.0 MB
    - Expandable Memory: microSD / TransFlash
- Imaging:
    - Main Screen: 65000 colors (TFT)
    - 176 x 220 px
    - External Screen: 65000 colors (TFT)
    - 96 x 96 px
    - Camera: 1.3 MP / 1280 x 960 px / Rotate / 4X Zoom / Multi-Shot / Self-Timer / Video Recorder / Video Calling
- Audio:
    - MP3 Player: MP3 / AAC / AAC+ / WMA / MusicID / 3D Stereo Sound
    - FM Radio: MobiRadio
    - Speakerphone: Yes
    - Push-To-Talk: N/A
- Multimedia:
    - Wallpapers: 176 x 220 px
    - Screen Savers: 176 x 220 px
    - Ring Tones: 72 chord / MP3
    - Themes: Yes
    - Games: Java ME
    - Streaming Multimedia: Cingular Video / MobiTV
- Messaging:
    - SMS: Yes
    - EMS: Yes
    - MMS: Yes

  - Email: AOL / Hotmail / Yahoo!
  - Chat: AOL / ICQ / MSN / Yahoo!
  - Predictive Text: T9
- Applications:
  - Phonebook Capacity: 500
  - Calendar: Yes
  - To-Do List: Yes
  - WAP:2.0
  - Voice Commands: N/A
  - Calculator: Yes
- Connectivity:
  - Bluetooth: A2DP / DUN / HFP / HSP / OPP
  - Infrared Port: N/A
  - High-Speed Data: HSDPA
  - Wi-Fi: N/A
  - GPS: N/A
  - PC Sync: USB Mass Storage

External links

- LG CU500v [1]

LG Trax (CU575)

LG Trax (CU575)

Manufacturer	LG
Carrier	AT&T
Available	2007
Screen	65K color TFT, 176x220 pixels, 11 lines
Exterior screen	65K color TFT, 128x160 pixels, 9 lines
Camera	1.3 MP, 1280 x 960, 640x480, 320x240, 160x120 pixels
Memory	16 MB
Memory card	microSD
Networks	GSM/GPRS/EDGE: 850/900/1800/1900 MHz WCDMA (HSDPA/UMTS): 850/1900 MHz
Connectivity	Bluetooth
Battery	Li-polymer, 980 mAh
Physical size	3.89" x 2.01" x 0.62"
Weight	3.55 oz
Form factor	Clamshell

The **LG CU575**, also known as the **Trax**, is a GSM/UMTS mobile phone carried by AT&T Mobility. It is designed to run on AT&T's UMTS frequencies of 850 and 1900 MHz. The phone features a slim design similar to the Motorola RAZR series, and also features external music controls and a microSD memory card slot supporting cards up to 4 GB. The phone is a replacement for the LG CU500.

External links

- LG Trax Product Page [1]

LG Secret (KF750)

LG Secret (KF750)

Manufacturer	LG Electronics
Available	Europe (May 3, 2008)
Screen	240 x 320, 2.4" Display 262K-color TFT LCD
Camera	5.0 megapixels Autofocus Schneider-Kreuznach Macro Mode Face detection
Operating system	Java MIDP 2.0
Default ringtone	Polyphonic, MP3
Memory	100 MB Internal
Memory card	MicroSD (TransFlash), up to 8GB
Networks	GSM 900/1800/1900 HSDPA/UMTS
Connectivity	Bluetooth V 2.0 USB 3G GPRS HSDPA 3.6 Mbit/s
Battery	800mAh Li-Ion
Physical size	102.8 x 50.8 x 11.8 mm
Weight	116g
Form factor	Slider
Series	Black Label Series
Predecessor	LG Shine
Related	Official Secret Website [1]

The **LG Secret** (a.k.a. **LG KF750**) is a 3G slider-style mobile phone manufactured by LG Electronics. It is the third phone in LG's "Black Label Series", following the *LG Chocolate* and *LG Shine*. It was released on May 3, 2008 in Europe. It has a 5.0 megapixel camera and Neon touch navigation, and is notable for incoporating these in a slim slider form design.

Design

The phone is black, with the battery cover made of carbon fiber. The front display is shielded with tempered glass. The top of the phone is covered with synthetic leather. The phone also features mechanical *Send*, *End* and *Cancel* buttons, addressing a complaint that some users had with previous LG phones.

Features

The phone is the world's slimmest 5.0 megapixel camera phone. It records video in VGA @ 30fps and QVGA @ 120fps and "time lapse videos". the QVGA videos are recorded in 120fps and then saved at 15fps. this enables slow motion videos. The videos are recorded with divx encoding which balances quality with file size.

It comes with a LED flash, which despite not being a xenon flash, functions well in dim lighting for objects up to 2 meters away. the phone also has support for divx videos. LG Secret comes with an accelerometer, which auto-adjusts the phone's display based on the orientation of the phone. The phone also comes with accelorometer games. The LG Secret comes with Auto Luminance Control which automatically adjusts screen brightness according to ambient brightness.

Price

The phone was sold in the UK market at launch for £339.95.

External links

- Official website of LG Secret (LG KF750) [2]
- LG Mobile Phone Page (LG KF750) [3]
- LG Secrets Review [4]

LG Black Label Series

LG Black Label Series

Black Label Series is a mobile phone series created by LG Electronics. Currently, there are 3 released versions:

- LG Chocolate (KG800) (International version) - May 2006
  LG Chocolate (VX8500) (US Version) - July, 2006
- LG Shine - 2007
- LG Secret - May 3, 2008
- New Chocolate - 2009
- A fourth edition of the black label series has been confirmed. A leaked promotional video for the 4th Black Label series (BL40) reveals a 4 inch tempered glass capacitive touchscreen with a 21:9 aspect ratio. The phone will run on a revamped edition of LG's S-class touch interface. Other features include GPS, A-GPS, 7.2 MBPS HSPDA, WIFI and a 5 MP camera.

External links

- LG Electronics Global Website [1]
- LG Electronics Korea Website [2]
- LG Mobile Website [1]
- "Life's Good When..." LG Video Contest [3]
- LG Video Contest YouTube Channel [4]

LG enV2 (VX9100)

LG enV2 (VX9100)

Manufacturer	LG Electronics
Carrier	Verizon Wireless
Available	March 31, 2008
Screen	2.4 in. (320 x 240 px) TFT LCD (260K Color)
Exterior screen	1.45 in. (160 x 64 px) TFT LCD (60K Color)
Camera	2 Megapixel
Input	QWERTY keyboard
Default ringtone	MP3
Memory	63 MB
Memory card	microSD
Networks	CDMA
Connectivity	Bluetooth 1.2 / microUSB
Battery	950 mAh Li-Pol
Physical size	3.75 in x 2.13 in x 0.65 in
Weight	4.23 ounces (120 g)
Form factor	Clamshell
Predecessor	enV (VX9900)
Successor	enV3 (VX9200)

Hearing aid compatibility	M3/T3

The **LG enV²** is a Verizon Wireless digital messaging phone manufactured by LG. It is available in standard black as well as maroon (pomegranate, in Canada). Both the colors are available at Verizon Wireless (Telus Stores and Koodo stores, in Canada) stores, and were released on the same date. It is also capable of installing VZ Navigator. The original price of the phone at release was $129 after a $50 mail-in-rebate. It had dropped to $79.99, and then to $49.99, but as of February 2009, the price has returned to $129.99. Best Buy stores also offer the enV² for a price of $49.99 with a 2 year contract.

It succeeded both the LG enV (VX9900) and the original LG The V (VX9800). The phone's successor, the LG enV3 (VX9200) was released in 2009.

The styling of this phone has been updated from the previous versions. It's slimmer (40% slimmer than original enV), lighter (30% lighter than original enV), and more pocketable than the previous versions. Its styling is made more comfortable and easier to handle and text, its shaped like a rectangle with both front and back of phone being a flat surface (unlike the original enV). The back of the phone is painted in SoftTouch paint in the phone's respective color (a smooth and grippy paint) making it more comfortable to handle. Its styling follows that of the LG Voyager (VX10000), which is the other successor to the LG enV (VX9900) and the LG The V (VX9800) phones. The Env2 was released in Canada in August, 2008 as the LG Keybo from Telus. Its successor, the enV3, was released on May 29, 2009.

Features

The enV² has several features, such as the QWERTY keyboard and a 2.0 megapixel camera with up to 10x zoom. It is Bluetooth-compatible and supports V CAST, Verizon's music and video service, as well as VZ Navigator, Verizon's map service. The phone has a microSD memory card port for storing music and video from a computer and is enabled to set videos under 5MB as wallpaper. It can store up to 300 text messages, has an "auto text readout" functionality(phone reads texts outloud for you), and message sorter. The phone supports FOTA, which allows for new firmware updates to be sent to the device without needing to make a trip to a retail store to receive the update.

The phone also has the capability to display four different themes which may change button styles, background colors, and general style of the phone. These themes are the Classic view, having the red and white menu screen when the OK button is pressed, the Slick Black theme, with a more digital, and of course, black look. There is also the Wall theme, with the menu and other features looking like a concrete wall. The last theme is the wave, a rounded and dark look.

The phone supports up to 8GB of storage via the MicroSD port on the right side of the phone. The forms of media able to be stored on this card include: Photos ("PIX"), Music, Sounds, and Videos ("FLIX"). This phone supports the Bluetooth profile A2DP which supports the listening of music through wireless headphones. The phone also has a "Standalone Mode" which allows one to take advantage of the phone's multimedia capabilities (Music, Photos, Videos, Games) without sending or receiving RF signals. This mode is most useful while on an airplane.

The phone has a full QWERTY keyboard optimized for text messaging, and comes in the alternate colors maroon and black.

Specific ringtones may be set for individual callers on the phone's contact list. However, unlike many previous LG models, it is not possible to set individual ringers for incoming TXT messages.

Specifications

The following are the specifications for the LG enV^2:

Type	Specification
Backlit Keypad	Yes
Battery Type	Lithium-Ion
Calculator	Yes
Calendar	Yes
Changeable Faceplate Capable	No
Customizable Ring Tones	Built-In, Downloadable
Data Capabilities	Yes
Extras	2.0MP Camera, Bluetooth, MP3 Player
Games	Yes, Downloadable
Hands-free Speakerphone	Yes
Included in Box	AC Charger Rechargeable Battery
Keypad Lock	Yes
Number of Display Lines	320 x 240 Pixels
Number of Modes/Bands	Dual band
Phone Book Capacity	1000
Product Dimensions	10.2(W) x 5.4(H) x 1.65(D) cm
Product Weight	120g
Standby Time	Up To 216 Hours
Supports Caller ID	Yes
Talk Time	Up to 5 hours
Vibrate Mode	Built-in

Web Browser	Yes

See also

- Helio Ocean
- LG Voyager (VX10000)
- LG enV (VX9900)
- LG The V (VX9800)
- Danger Hiptop (T-Mobile Sidekick)

External links

- *us.lge*: enV² [1]
- *Verizon Wireless*: "enV²" [2]
- *PhoneScoop*: LG enV² (VX-9100) [3]
- *Skatter Tech*: "LG enV2 (VX9100) Review" [4]
- LG Env2 Updates [5]
- *611Connect*: " LG enV² in Maroon or Black Cell Phone Reviews and Ratings" [6]

LG Rumor (LX260)

LG Rumor (LX260)

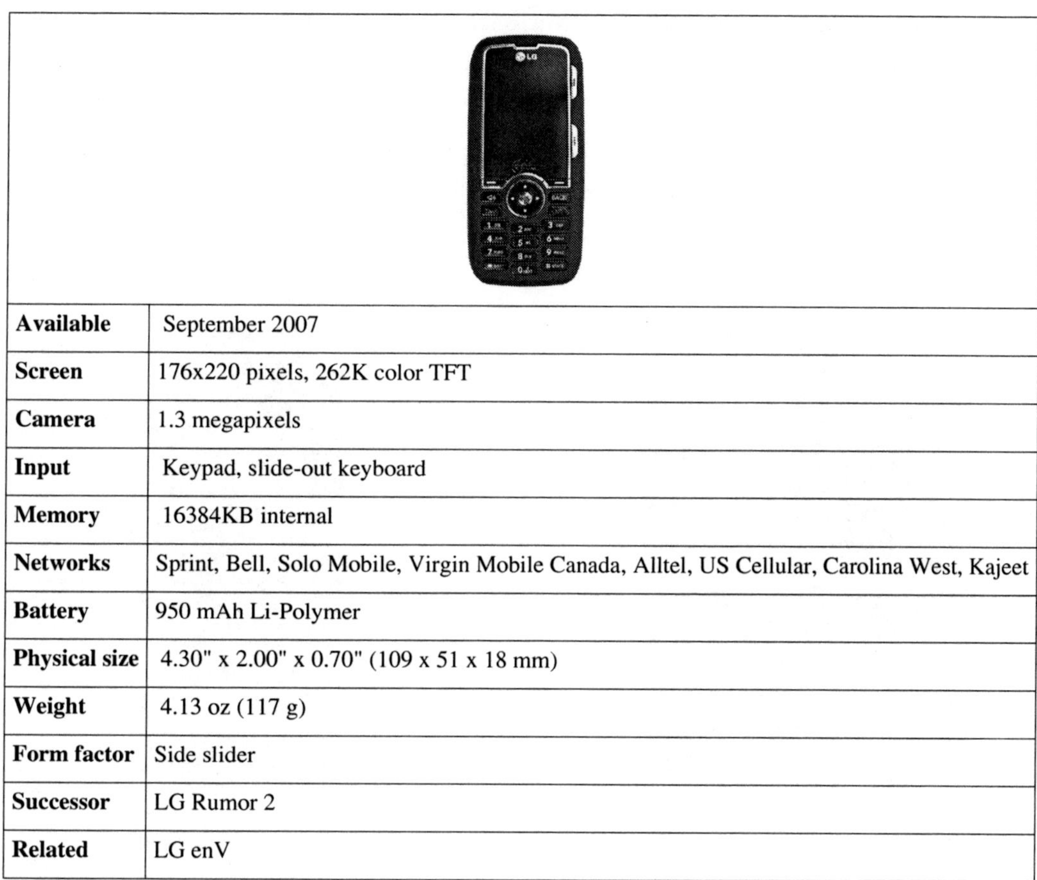

Available	September 2007
Screen	176x220 pixels, 262K color TFT
Camera	1.3 megapixels
Input	Keypad, slide-out keyboard
Memory	16384KB internal
Networks	Sprint, Bell, Solo Mobile, Virgin Mobile Canada, Alltel, US Cellular, Carolina West, Kajeet
Battery	950 mAh Li-Polymer
Physical size	4.30" x 2.00" x 0.70" (109 x 51 x 18 mm)
Weight	4.13 oz (117 g)
Form factor	Side slider
Successor	LG Rumor 2
Related	LG enV

The **LG LX260**, also known as the **LG Rumor** in the United States, **LG Rumour** and **LG Rumeur** in English and French Canadian markets, respectively, or **LG Scoop**, is a mobile phone released by LG Electronics in September 2007. The phone features a slide-out QWERTY keyboard in addition to the standard 12-button keypad, a 1.3 megapixel camera, and a 176x220 pixel screen.

Features

The LG Rumor/LG Scoop is a phone that was released by Sprint Nextel in September 2007 . This phone features a QWERTY keyboard that slides out from the right side. 5-way navigation keys are located on the main panel of the phone, but not present on the keyboard. A 176x220 pixel screen rotates as the keyboard is open, but has no contrast controls. The 1.3 megapixel camera lacks an LED flash and a self-portrait mirror but does have negative, sepia, black & white tones, borders and an image enhancer to customize a picture. Basic MP3 playing functions are embedded in this phone, with the capability of expanding music storage via MicroSD card (125 to 1,000 music files depending on file size, encoding method, and card capacity). The music player will not launch unless a card is inserted in the phone, and will not accept a card with the memory that is over 4 GB.

LG Rumor/LG Scoop can be connected with Bluetooth technology, (stores up to 20 Bluetooth entries), or a proprietary LG USB cable. It can hold 500 contacts with additional numbers, notes and email addresses.

Slide-out keyboard (in black)

Camera on back of phone (in black)

Specifications

Type	Specification
Modes	CDMA 800 / CDMA 1900
Weight	4.13 oz (117 g)
Dimensions	4.30" x 2.00" x 0.70" (109 x 51 x 18 mm)
Form Factor	Slide, Internal Antenna
Battery Life	Talk: 270 minutes, Standby: 240 hours
Battery Type	Li-Poly 950 mAh
Display	Type: LCD (Color TFT/TFD), 10 line, Colors: 262,144, Size: 176 x 220 pixels
Platform / OS	Brew MP
Memory	Phone internal: 16384KB, Additional MicroSD memory (up to 4 GB)
Phone Book Capacity	500
FCC ID	--
GPS / Location	Yes, enabled by default
Digital TTY/TDD	Yes
Hearing Aid Compatible	Rating: M3
Multiple Languages	English, Spanish,
Polyphonic Ringtones	Yes
Vibrate	Yes
Bluetooth	Supported Profiles: HFP, HSP, OPP, DUN, FTP, OBEX
Multiple Numbers per Name	Yes
Picture ID	Yes
Ringer ID	Yes, and text message ID
Voice Dialing	No
Custom Graphics	Yes
Custom Ringtones	Yes, for Sprint. No (custom ringtones available for purchase on Axcess Apps, standard on Alltel phones)
Data-Capable	Yes
Flight Mode	Yes
Packet Data	Technology: 1xRTT
WAP / Web Browser	Yes, dial up and USB tethered
Predictive Text Entry	Technology: T9 Predictive

Side Keys	Left side: Volume, Camera
Memory Card Slot	Card Type: MicroSD up to 4GB
MMS	Yes
Text Messaging	Yes, up to 140 characters, 25 recipients at a time
Text Messaging Templates	Yes (canned messages)
Music Player	Yes, Supported Formats: MP3, AAC, AAC+, M4A, MID
Camera	Resolution: 1.3 MP self-timer, night mode functions / brightness, white balance controls
Streaming Video	Yes
Video Capture	Yes, 15 second/256KB "Video Mail" clips, recording time varies by memory card size
Alarm	Yes
Calculator	Yes [basic], plus tip calculator
Calendar	Yes
Voice Memo	Yes, ability to record memo and calls
BREW	No
Games	Yes
Unit Converter	Yes

Availability

As the LG Rumor/LG Scoop became a popular phone for social teens and for business clients who require basic email support, it is currently sold by CDMA cellphone carriers in North America, such as Sprint, Bell Mobility, Solo Mobile, Virgin Mobile Canada, kajeet, US Cellular, and Alltel (known as LG Scoop).

There are different colors sold by different cellphone providers.

Rumor

- Black (Sprint, Bell, Solo, Virgin, US Cellular)
- White (Sprint, Bell, Virgin, Solo, US Cellular)
- Lime Green (Sprint, Virgin)
- Orange (Solo)
- Blue (Virgin, Sprint)
- Purple (Carolina West Wireless)

Scoop

- Turquoise (Alltel)
- Lavender (Alltel, Virgin)

- Red (Alltel)
- Slate/Black (Alltel)
- Citrus/Orange (Alltel)
- Grey (Carolina West Wireless)

Rumor^2

In early 2009 LG & Sprint offered a new, updated version of the Rumor called the LG Rumor 2 with a 4 row QWERTY keyboard instead of a 3-row keyboard. Also, a new interface and IM-like text messaging interface debuted. However, the Rumor 2 does not include video recording capabilities that the original Rumor has. It is not currently offered on Sprint's online store because of the recent release of the LG Rumor Touch.

Rumor Touch

In early 2010 LG & Sprint offered a new, updated version of the Rumor^2 called the LG Rumor Touch with a 5 row QWERTY keyboard instead of 3 row rumor or 4 row Rumor^2. It also includes a touch screen. It is currently offered at $29.99 with a two year contract from Sprint. The Rumor Touch does include video recording capabilities that the Rumor has, but the Rumor^2 did not include.

LG Dare (VX9700)

LG Dare (VX9700)

Available	2008
Screen	3inch./240x400 resolution/262K colors
Default ringtone	MP3
Memory	200 MB, 28 MB RAM
Networks	CDMA
Connectivity	Bluetooth / USB Cable
Physical size	4.1"H x 2.2"W x 0.5"D
Weight	3.76 oz
Hearing aid compatibility	M3/T3

The **LG VX9700** (or "LG Dare") is a CDMA touch screen cell phone made by LG. The phone features touch screen navigation, a 3.2 megapixel camera with face recognition and many photo enhancing tools, a camcorder, customizable shortcut menus, handwriting recognition, and a multitask music player. The LG Dare is the third phone to have Rev. A technology - after the Sprint Mogul and Touch.

In the US, the Dare was released online June 26, 2008 and was released in Verizon stores on July 3, 2008. The device is available in Canada on the Telus Mobility network.

Display and menus

The TFT screen has a resolution of 240x400 pixels and can display 262,144 colors. When waiting for input, the phone displays its Standby screen or turns off the screen and disables the touchscreen. When charging, the phone can display a slideshow, a "desk clock", a calendar, or nothing.

The Standby screen displays the network type, signal strength, Location setting, and battery condition across the top. The background of the screen can be set to a slide show of images, a Flash animation, a video, or an image. The Standby screen can also display a translucent date/time bar of your choosing.

Across the bottom is the Softkey menu, a set of five icons that provide easy access to important features: Messaging, Call, Menu, Phonebook, and Favorites. Touching the background or the Shortcut Menu on the right side of the phone brings up a customizable menu with 11 icons. A shortcut can be set to a program (including downloaded ones), a menu, a library, and other features on the phone.

Connectivity and power

The Dare works on a dual-band CDMA cell network and is 3G capable. It also has a stereo 2.1 Bluetooth radio, and can access the internet through the cellular connection. Besides the Dare's 200MB internal memory, it has a flash memory slot for microSD or microSDHC, supporting cards up to 16GB in size. The phone also supports GPS, PIM, and BREW, as well.

The phone has a 3.5mm stereo jack for headphones, and a microUSB connector for syncing with a PC and charging. The Dare retail box comes with a USB cable and an AC charging brick with a USB port for connecting the cable. The battery capacity is 1100mAh and is rated for up to 4.66 hours (280 minutes) of talk time, or up to 360 hours (15 days) on stand-by.

Phone calls and phone book

To make calls, one can press the phone icon on the softkey bar or the phonebook icon. Pressing the phone icon brings up a standard 12-key alphanumeric keypad, as well as options for speaking or drawing the number.

Pressing the phonebook icon brings up the phonebook. This list is alphabetized and has an alphabetical index across the top for quick access. Also at the top is quick access to ICE information (ICE is an acronym for **I**n **C**ase of **E**mergency and is used in cell phones to indicate emergency contact information to a third party). The phonebook can store multiple numbers, email addresses, and other information for each contact, including a personalized image and ringtone option.

The Dare also has a feature which allows the user to save a list of their favorite contacts and have quick access to them. This Favorites menu is accessible through the star icon on the softkey bar.

Camera

The LG Dare has a 3.2 megapixel camera with a Schneider-Kreuznach autofocus lens and an LED flash. Some features of the camera include 5 different resolutions, five white balance presets, five color effects, four ISO settings (Auto ISO, ISO 100, ISO 200, and ISO 400), digital zoom (not available on highest resolution) and six preset scenes. Other options include multishot, shutter sounds (three of them), auto focus, self timer, and four different shot types (Normal, Panorama, Split and Frame). An innovative feature called SmartPic offers face detection and enhances images with face color compensation.

The camcorder function provides two quality options and several resolutions to allow the user to save high-quality video or lower resolutions suited for sending over MMS. The video camera has the ability to digital zoom. The Dare is one of the first phones available in the US to record in high speed.

Messaging and text input

The Dare supports EMS, MMS, SMS, and Instant Messaging. For this and any other text inputs, the phone provides several options. One can bring up a standard keypad with letters and use multi-tap (T9 (predictive text)) or a word-guessing system. If the phone is turned sideways, it senses the change in orientation and brings up a full keyboard. Also of note is a handwriting feature which allows the user to write numbers or letters by writing with a finger. In each of these modes, the user must manually change the setting (capital or lowercase letters, numbers, or symbols) to allow the phone to know what type of character is being input.

Ringtones and multimedia playback

The phone uses MP3 polyphonic and Truetone ringtones and has vibrate options. It also plays videos and music in MP3, AAC (unprotected only) , AAC+, and WMA formats.

Specs

LG Dare specifications

Category	Sub-Category	Info	Notes
Network	*Type*	CDMA dual band (800/1900 MHz)	
	Data	CDMA2000 1xRTT/1xEV-DO rev.0/1xEV-DO rev.A	
	3G Capable	Yes	
Size	*Dimensions*	4.1h x 2.2w x .5d	
	Weight	3.8 oz (107 g)	
Design	*Form*	Candybar	
	Antenna	Internal	
Battery	*Type*	Li - Ion	
	Talk	Up to 4.66 (280 mins) hours of Talk Time	
	Standby	Up to 360 hours (15 days) of Stand-by Time	
	Capacity	1100 mAh	
Main Display	*Resolution*	240 x 400 pixels	
	Type	262 144 colors, TFT	
	Features	Light and Proximity Sensors	
	Touch Screen	Resistive	

Camera	*Resolution*	3.2 megapixels Resolution	
	Video	VGA (640x480)	
	Features	Flash: Yes, Schneider Kreuznach lens, Digital zoom	
Notifications	*Polyphonic Ringtones*	Yes, MP3	
	Vibration Alert	Yes	
Messaging	*Text Send/Receive*	Yes	
	EMS	Yes	
	MMS	Yes	
	Instant Messaging	Yes	
Multimedia	*Video Playback*	Video player for MP4, 3GP, 3G2 Formats	
	Music Player	MP3, AAC, AAC+, WMA formats supported	
Memory	*Memory Slot*	microSD/microSDHC (up to 16gb), 200mb internal memory	
Connectivity	*Internet*	Full HTML browser	3g2/AAC Audio/Video web browser player
	USB	microUSB	
	Bluetooth	Stereo 2.1, yes (also works with movies and GPS)	
	Connectors	HeadPhone Jack (3.5mm)	
Other Features	*PhoneBook*	1000 contacts, Caller groups supported, Multiple Numbers Per Contact, Picture ID, Ring ID	
	PIM	Alarm, Calendar, Calculator, TO-DO, Stopwatch, World Clock, Notebook, Notepad & Drawing Pad with handwriting recognition	
	Voice	Recording, Speaker Phone	
	BREW	Yes	
	Email	Yes	
	GPS	Yes	
	FCC Approved	Yes	

See also

- LG Prada (KE850)
- LG Vu

Sources

- Dare by LG [1]
- LG Dare (Verizon Wireless) [2]
- LG Dare Updates [3]
- LG VX9700 looks to be Verizon's Prada-like touchscreen phone [4]
- Update 4 with picture: LG VX9700 is Verizon's PRADA-like phone (Phone Arena) [5]
- LG Dare at WikiSpecs [6]-Detailed Specsheet
- FCC Link [7]
- IntoMobile.com leak of July 4th 2008 release [8]

LG Vu (CU915/CU920)

LG Vu (CU915/CU920)

Manufacturer	LG
Carrier	AT&T, Rogers
Screen	262K Color TFT, 240 x 400 Pixels, 3.00" (touch screen)
Camera	2.0 Megapixel with video capability
Input	Touch Screen
CPU	400 MHz
Memory	152798 KB
Memory card	microSD
Networks	GSM, 3G
Connectivity	Bluetooth 2.1
Battery	1,000 mAh Li-Ion
Physical size	4.25" (H) x 2.16" (W) x 0.51" (D)
Weight	3.16 oz.
Form factor	Bar phone
Predecessor	LG Prada

The **LG Vu** (CU915/CU920) is a touchscreen feature phone made by LG. The phone is on the AT&T network and the CU920 features mobile TV. In Canada, a variant was sold under the model name TU915 by Rogers and Fido.

Features

LG Vu specifications

Category	Sub-Category	Info
Network	*Type*	GSM Quad-band (850/900/1800/1900 MHz)
	Data	GPRS/EDGE, UMTS/HSDPA (850/1900 MHz)
	3G Capable	Yes
Size	*Dimensions*	4.25h x 2.16w x .51d
	Weight	3.16 oz (90 g)
Design	*Form*	Candybar
	Antenna	Internal
Battery	*Type*	Li-Ion
	Talk	Up to 3 hours (180 minutes) of Talk Time
	Standby	Up to 250 hours (10 days and 10 hours) of Stand-by Time
	Capacity	1,000 mAh
Main Display	*Resolution*	240 x 400 pixels
	Type	262,144 colors, TFT
	Features	Locking screen
	Touch Screen	Yes
Camera	*Resolution*	2.0 megapixels Resolution with video
	Video	QVGA (320x240)
	Features	Flash: No, Schneider Kreuznach lens, Digital zoom
Notifications	*Polyphonic Ringtones*	Yes, MP3
	Vibration Alert	Yes
Messaging	*Text Send/Receive*	Yes
	EMS	Yes
	MMS	Yes
	Instant Messaging	Yes
Multimedia	*Video Playback*	Video player
	Music Player	MP3, AAC, AAC+, EAAC+, WMA formats supported, XM Radio
Memory	*Memory Slot*	microSD/microSDHC, 150MB (120MB available) internal memory

Connectivity	*Internet*	Full HTML browser
	USB	Yes
	Bluetooth	Yes, 2.1
	Connectors	Proprietary LG Connector
Other Features	*PhoneBook*	1000 contacts, Caller groups supported, Multiple Numbers Per Contact, Picture ID, Ring ID
	PIM	Alarm, Calendar, Calculator, Task List, Stopwatch, World Clock, Notepad, Tip Calculator, Unit Converter
	Voice	Recording, Speaker Phone, Command
	BREW	Yes
	Email	Yes
	GPS	No
	FCC Approved	Yes

Interface

Most of the features on the Vu are accessed through its 3" diagonal touch screen. The phone has Call, Clear and End buttons below the screen, and a volume rocker, Lock/Unlock button, and camera button along the right side. The Vu also contains haptic feedback which is a vibration felt when the touch screen is touched.This phone also had a nickname "pressure screen" because of how non sensitive the screen is compared to the leading touch screen phones. Like the popular LG Prada, it has the famous fish or butterfly following the touch of your finger on the screen.

External links

- LG Electronics [1]-LG Official Website
- LG-Vu.com [2] - A Forum about LG Vu
- LG Vu at WikiSpecs [3]
- MobileTechReview.com [4] - Detailed phone review
- Featured in PCWorld.ca's [4] round-up of Top Canadian Smartphones and Cell Phones [5]

LG KU 380

LG KU 380

Manufacturer	LG
Screen	256 colors, 176x220 pixels
Camera	1.3MP, 1280x960
Memory	60Mb
Memory card	MicroSD
Weight	91g

The **LG KU380** is a slide phone made by LG and hosted by Vodafone. The slide phone has two cameras, one in the front top right side and the other camera is on the back similar to most other slide phones. It is available in two colors, white and black. The keyboard of the phone is flat. The camera is 1.3 Megapixels.

Codes for LG KU380

- 3845#*380# - Test mode
- 2945#*380# - Lock/Unlock menu

Includes:		
Camera,	VideoPhone	Memorycard slot
3G Internet,	E-Mail,	row 2,

LG Chocolate (VX8560)

LG Chocolate (VX8560)

Available	2008
Screen	LCD 240 × 320 pixels (262144 colors)
Default ringtone	MP3
Memory	1 GB (internal)
Networks	CDMA
Connectivity	Bluetooth / USB cable
Physical size	3.87 × 1.94 × 0.64 inches
Weight	3.36 oz
Successor	LG Chocolate Touch

The **LG Chocolate**[3] (also known as the **VX8560** or the upgraded **VX8560EX** with differences such as a 2 Mp camera) is a feature phone, and the upgrade to the popular LG Chocolate music phone for Verizon Wireless in the USA and Telus in Canada. It was released online July 14, 2008 and comes in black (dark blue) and baby blue (light blue). The phone has many enhancements over the original VX8500 Chocolate series such as a clam shell (flip) design, an external display, a change in the key layout, an updated music player, a smoother design, and a built-in FM transmitter.

Here the LG Chocolate[3] is shown playing music using the external screen.

Specifications

The complete LG VX8560 list of specifications are:

Type	Specification Average cost at store - $99.99 after $50 mail-in rebate. (As of November 2008)
Modes	CDMA 800 / CDMA 1900 (Digital Dual-Band)
Weight	3.36 oz
Dimensions	3.87" × 1.94" × .64"
Form factor	Clamshell - internal antenna
Battery life	Talk: up to 270 minutes (≈3+ hours) / Standby: up to 350 hours (≈14+ days)
Battery type	Lithium Ion 800 mAh (1500 mAH optional battery available)
Display	Type: LCD (color TFT/TFD) Colors: 262,144 (18-bit) Size: 240 × 320 pixels
Platform / OS	Qualcomm BREW 3.1.5.145 Software: 2.0.5.v1)
Memory	1 GB (built-in, flash shared memory)
Phone Book Capacity	1000
2nd Display	Location: Front 260,000-color TFT LCD / 220 × 176 pixels
Alarm	Yes
Bluetooth	version 2.1+EDR (Enhanced Date Rate)/ Headset, Hands–Free, Dial–Up networking, Advanced Audio Distribution (stereo), Phonebook Access, Basic Printing, Object Push for vCard and Calendar, File Transfer and Basic Imaging
BREW	Yes
Java	No
Calculator	Yes (includes Tip Calculator)
Calendar	Yes
Camera	Resolution: 1.3 (or 2.0 with the VX8560EX) megapixel no-flash / self-timer, night mode, macro mode func

Custom graphics	Yes
Custom ringtones	Yes
Data-capable	Yes
Digital TTY/TDD	Yes
EMS / Picture Messaging	Yes
Expansion card	Card type: microSD
Games	Yes
GPS / Location	Yes
Headset jack (3.5 mm)	Yes (Note: This is a headphone (3.5 mm or 1/8 inch) jack for use with ears buds and the like.)
Hearing Aid compatible	Rating: M3 (mostly compatible)
High-Speed data	Technology: 1xEV-DO r0
Low-Speed Data	"Quick 2 Net" (QNC): unsupported
Media Center	Software Version: 3.1.5.145
MMS	Yes
Multiple Languages	Languages Supported: English, Spanish
Multiple Numbers per Name	Numbers per entry: 5 plus 2 email addresses
Music Player	Supported Formats: MP3 with equalizer
Music Transmitter	Built-in FM Transmitter 87.5 MHz - 107.9 MHz
Picture ID	Yes
Polyphonic Ringtones	Chords: 72
Predictive Text Entry	Technology: T9
Side Keys	on left and right when closed
Speaker Phone	Type: Full-Duplex
Streaming Multimedia	Yes
Text Messaging	2-Way: Yes
USB	Yes

Vibrate	Yes
Video capture	Yes
Voice Dialing	speaker-independent / plus voice command and text-to-speech
Voice Memo	Number of entries: 200 up to 1 minute or 60 minute each
Wireless Internet	Browser software: Openwave 6.2.3.2

LG VX8100

LG VX8100

Manufacturer	LG
Carrier	Verizon Wireless Telus
Available	July 15, 2005
Screen	18-bit 176x220
Exterior screen	16-bit 128x128
Camera	1.3 megapixel
Memory card	MiniSD
Weight	4.16 oz
Predecessor	LG VX8000
Successor	LG VX8300
Hearing aid compatibility	M3/T3

The **LG VX8100** is a mobile phone that was available through Verizon Wireless in 2005 and 2006. It used Verizon's EV-DO network and was one of the first phones to support V CAST service. It also featured Bluetooth capability, stereo speakers, and a MiniSD slot.

Reception

The VX8100 received mix reviews. Some compared it unfavorably to its predecessor, the VX8000, because the VX8100 was heavier, had a shorter battery life, a protruding antenna, a smaller screen, and did not include an analog compatibility mode Another source of criticism was that there were four different firmware versions of the phone—none of which were marked on the box—which made for inconsistent consumer experiences.

However, Laptop magazine rated it 4 out of 5 stars, mostly based on its multimedia functionality and faster data rate.

Based on call quality, features, and durability the VX8100 continues to retain a great fan base 5 years after initial launch.

Detailed Specs

- Network: CDMA 800/1900
- Main LCD: 18-bit 176x220
- External LCD: 16-bit 128x128
- Camera: 1.3 megapixel, 8x digital zoom, 1280x960

External links

- VX8100 Service Menu Information [1]
- Mobiledia [2]

LG KS20

LG KS20

Manufacturer	LG Electronics
Available	2007
Screen	262K color TFT touchscreen, 2.8", 240 x 320 (QVGA)
Camera	2.0 megapixel, video QVGA@15fps, Strobe Flash
Second camera	VGA Video call (Front)
Memory	128 MB
Memory card	MicroSD
Networks	HSDPA, GSM / GPRS / EDGE Tri-Band (900/1800/1900)
Connectivity	Bluetooth 1.2, USB 2.0
Physical size	99.8 x 58 x 12.8 mm (L x W x D)
Weight	92.5 grams
Form factor	Candybar

The **LG-KS20** is a touch screen mobile phone with a stylish pitch black & minimal design manufactured by LG Electronics. It was released in Europe on November 7, 2007.

Features

LG KS20 provides customers with an advanced mobile Internet experience with its WiFi, 2.8 inch large screen, intuitive touch input and light portable with only 12.8mm thickness.

Compatible with the current broadband mobile internet standard, the phone allows users to enjoy the full benefits of 3.6 Mbit/s mobile internet, downloading of music, video clips and Windows Live content, as well as push e-mail. Application of the 2.8 inch large screen and landscape function with optimum convenience to enjoy video clips and internet surfing experience.

Specification sheet

Model LG KS20		
Group	**Functionality**	**Status**
Basic Specification	• Network band • Data band • Dimension: L x W x D (mm) • Weight with Battery, Standard (g) • Standard Battery, Max (mAh) • Standby Time, Max (hrs) • Talk Time (hrs) • Display External LCD (Pixel) • No. of Color • Vibrative Alert • SIM Toolkit • Data/Fax	• GSM900/1800/1900/WCDMA2100 • GPRS/EDGE/UMTS/HSDPA • 99.8 x 58 x 12.8 • 92.5g • 1050 mAh • 400hrs • 2hr 40min • 240 x 320 (2.8 inch QVGA LCD) Touchscreen • 262K • Yes • Yes • Yes/No
Internet	• Browser • WAP	• IE mobile 7.6 • version 2.0
Messaging	• SMS/MMS • Video MMS • Predictive Text Input (T9) • Instant Messaging • Download/Save as Support	• Yes/Yes • Yes • Yes (Word complete) • Yes • Yes
Voice/Data Connectivity	• Voice Memo • Video Telephony • IrDA • USB/PC Sync • WLAN • Bluetooth	• Yes • Yes • No • Yes/Yes • WiFi 802.11 b/g • 2.0+EDR, A2DP
PIM	• Scheduler/Alarm • Phonebook (# of names)	• Yes/Yes • Unlimited
Personalization	• Wallpaper/Screensaver • Picture/Ring Tone Downloading	• Yes/Yes • Yes/Yes

Advance Features	• OS • JAVA 9 Version • MIDI (Play) • FM Radio • Key Tone Effect • Built-in Camera (# of Games) • VOD/AOD • Video Recording / Video Capture • Camera (Main/Sub) • Internal Memory • External Memory • Multi-Media Players • Document Viewer	• Microsoft Windows Mobile 6.0 • MIDP 2.0 • 72 • Yes • Yes - Intuitive touch input • Windows App 2.0 • Seamless video streaming/Fast music downloads • Yes/Yes • 2.0 Mega Pixel Auto Focus Camera CMOS/VGA camera for video calling • 128MB RAM/256MB ROM • MicroSD up to 2GB • MP3, MPEG4, WAV, 3GP, AMR-NB, WMA, MIDI, AAC, AAC+, eAAC+ • MS Office (editable)
Customized Mobile UI	Today screen plug-in short-cut button, LC Menu program provided and with Windows Live support	
PS Note	Powerful utility with which user can compose a multimedia inserted document and image easily using the natural handwriting recognition	
Preloaded Application	Plus 3rd parties downloadable free applications	
Accessories	Battery • Stylus • Travel Adapter • Ear Mic (call button type) • Data CD	

See also

- Touchscreen
- HTC Touch Diamond
- iPhone
- Samsung Omnia

External links

- Official Website [1]
- LG KS20 CNET Asia Review [2]
- LG KS20 review [3]

LG Renoir (KC910)

LG Renoir (KC910)

The **LG KC910 Renoir** is a feature phone released by LG Electronics.The LG renoir is the world's first ***full touchscreen eight-megapixel*** cameraphone. It debuted in the fourth quarter of 2008. It has an 8-megapixel camera with xenon flash and Schneider Kreuznach optics.

Specifications

Feature	Specification
Form factor	Slate
Operating System	LG
2G/GSM frequencies	850 / 900 / 1800 / 1900
3G/HSDPA frequencies	HSDPA 900 / 2100 (850 / 1900 - American version), connections up to 7.2 Mbit/s
GPRS	Class 10 (4+1/3+2 slots), 32 - 48 kbit/s
EDGE (EGPRS)	Yes
WCDMA	No
HSCSD	No
Screen	TFT WQVGA LCD touchscreen, Flash UI, 240 x 400 pixels, 3.0 inches
Graphics	240 x 400 pixels, 256K colors
Audio	Dolby mobile

Accelerometer	Yes
CPU	140 MHz
Internal Dynamic Memory (RAM)	100 MB
Internal Flash Memory	
Camera features	8 MP, **Schneider Kreuznach** optics, Xenon flash ,3264x2448 pixels, autofocus, ISO sensitivity up to 1600, stabilization, auto-focus, manual focus, Face Tracking, Smile Shot, blink detection, geotagging, creative shot modes
Camera Lens Cover	Yes
Video recording	VGA 30fps, QVGA 5fps up to 120fps (640x384 Max.resolution)
Video call	Yes, secondary VGA videocall camera
Messaging	SMS, EMS, MMS, Email
Push to talk	
Java support	MIDP 2.0
Memory card slot	microSD (TransFlash), up to 8GB
Call Records	40 dialed, 40 received, 40 missed calls
GPS	Embedded GPS receiver
Bluetooth	Yes, v2.0 with A2DP
WLAN	Wi-Fi 802.11b/g
Infrared port	No
USB	Yes, v2.0
Data cable support	Yes
Browser	WAP 2.0/xHTML, HTML
Email	Yes
Push e-mail	Yes
Vibration	Yes
Ringtones	Polyphonic, MP3
Music player	MP3/MPEG4/AAC
Radio	FM Radio
Video playback formats	DivX/Xvid/MP4
Audio playback formats	MP3/WMA/AAC

Integrated speakers	Yes
TV out	Yes
HF speakerphone	Yes
Battery	Li-Ion 1000 mAh
Talk time	3 hours
Standby time	264 hours
Weight	114 g / 0.25 lbs
Dimensions	107.8 x 55.9 x 14 mm / 4.24" x 2.2" x 0.55"
Navigation	Yes

LG Cookie (KP500)

LG Cookie (KP500)

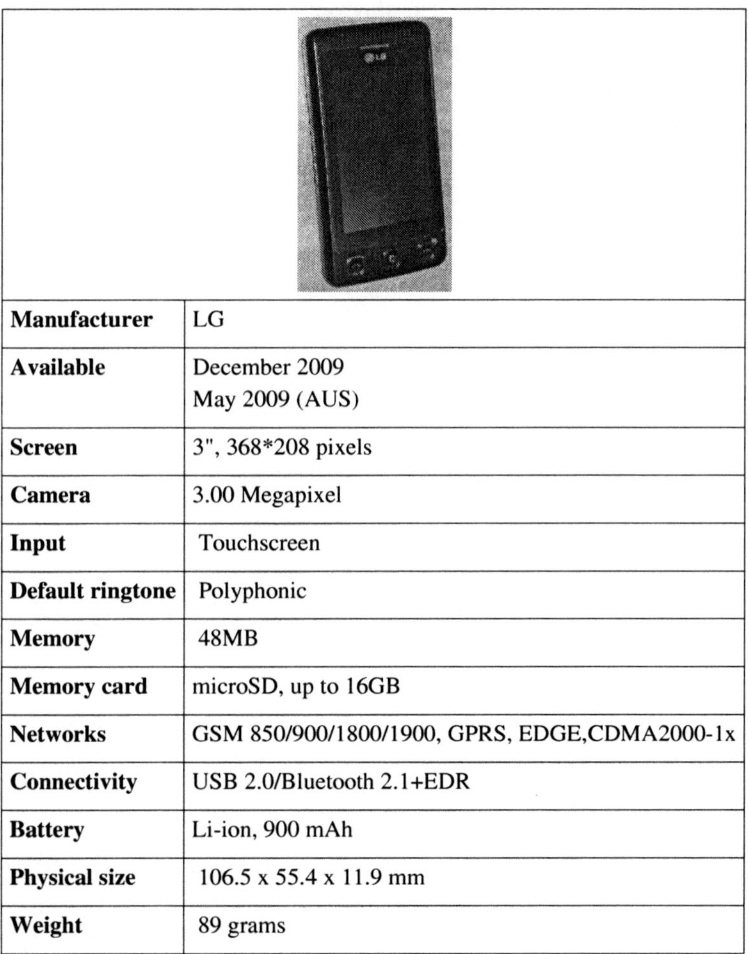

Manufacturer	LG
Available	December 2009 May 2009 (AUS)
Screen	3", 368*208 pixels
Camera	3.00 Megapixel
Input	Touchscreen
Default ringtone	Polyphonic
Memory	48MB
Memory card	microSD, up to 16GB
Networks	GSM 850/900/1800/1900, GPRS, EDGE,CDMA2000-1x
Connectivity	USB 2.0/Bluetooth 2.1+EDR
Battery	Li-ion, 900 mAh
Physical size	106.5 x 55.4 x 11.9 mm
Weight	89 grams

The **KP500** (nicknamed **LG Cookie**) is a touchscreen mobile phone. LG targeted the entry-level touchscreen market keeping the cost of the KP500 as low as possible by omitting some of the features found on high-end products, such as GPS, 3G or Wi-Fi. For example, in the UK, the KP500 is available for less than £50 in some stores.

The LG KP500 has recorded over two million unit sales worldwide in the five months since its launch in December 2008. It has sold 1.2 million units in Europe, 600,000 units in Asia and emerging markets, and 100,000 in Korea, where LG claims that as of March 2009, it is the most popular handset.

The phone was originally released in four colors including Black, Vandyke Brown, Anodizing Silver, and Elegant Gold, but is now available in ten colors, most common four are black, white, pink and most recent, purple, with more planned. LG plans to expand the KP500's availability from 40 to 60 countries as part of its push to hit 10 million in sales worldwide.

Its main feature is a 3-inch, 240 x 400 pixel touchscreen. The KP500 also contains an accelerometer motion sensor with support for auto-rotating display. It has a 3.15 MP Camera with MPEG-4 video capture at 12 frame/s. There is support for video playback up to 29 frames per second. The KP500 has a FM radio with RDS. Other software include a document viewer for DOC, XLS, and PDF formats, and a Java MIDP 2.0 games player.

Standby time is up to 350 hours and talk time is up to 3 hours 30 minutes.

External links

- Official LG KP500 website [1]
- Stress test of a cell phone LG KP500 [2]
- Un-Official LG KP500 Support Forum [3]
- LG KP500 PC SUITE Direct Download Link [4]

LG KS360

LG KS360

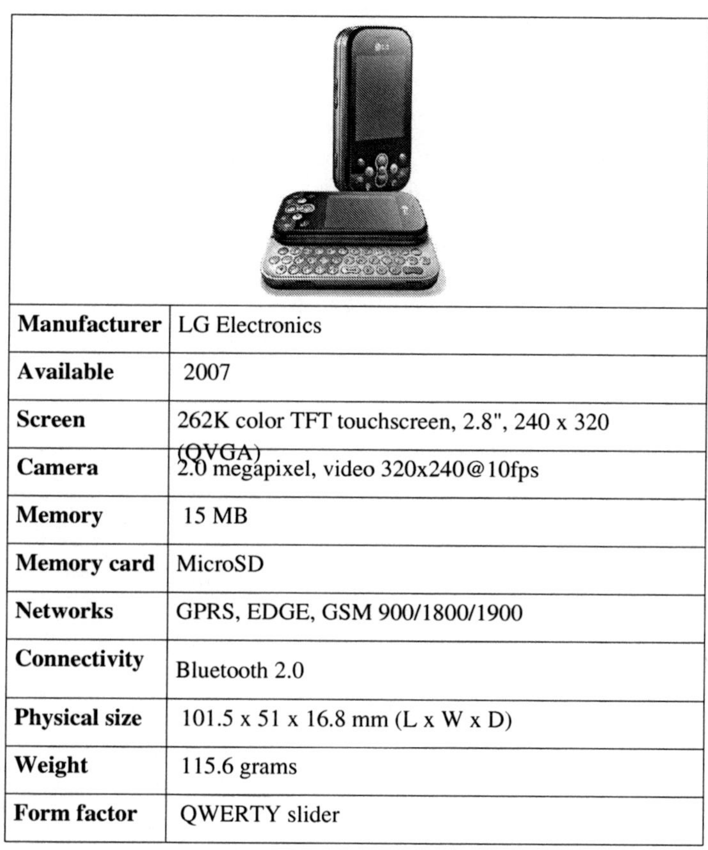

Manufacturer	LG Electronics
Available	2007
Screen	262K color TFT touchscreen, 2.8", 240 x 320 (QVGA)
Camera	2.0 megapixel, video 320x240@10fps
Memory	15 MB
Memory card	MicroSD
Networks	GPRS, EDGE, GSM 900/1800/1900
Connectivity	Bluetooth 2.0
Physical size	101.5 x 51 x 16.8 mm (L x W x D)
Weight	115.6 grams
Form factor	QWERTY slider

Features

The phone is geared towards text messaging and social networking, with a full QWERTY keyboard and a threaded conversation view for faster texting. It also has a heat sensitive screen which can be used for dialing numbers. The phone can use MicroSD cards of up to 4GB in size. The phone has Bluetooth 2.0, and WAP and GPRS are used to connect to the internet. Aimed at the youth market, the phone is available in black with blue, light pink and black, black and silver and red and pink.

The phone also has a numeric keypad.

External links

- User WEB page [1] How to program in BASIC on your LG Phone!

LG GD910

LG GD910

Manufacturer	LG Electronics
Carrier	Orange
Available	Q4 2009
Screen	1.43" QQVGA
Camera	Yes
Operating system	LG's Flash-Based OS
Input	Touchscreen + Side buttons
Networks	GSM 850/900/1800/1900, GPRS Class 10, EDGE, HSDPA 7.2 Mbit/s
Connectivity	Bluetooth 2.0
Physical size	61 x 39 x 13.9 mm
Weight	84g
Form factor	Watch

The **LG-GD910** is a quad-band 3G watch phone that has a touchscreen and video calling capabilities; manufacturer LG Electronics claims it is the first market-ready example of such a device. The world's first watch phone was a Samsung SPH-WP10 in 1999.

It was developed from a prototype that the company first demonstrated in 2008. The LG-GD910 was first publicly shown at CES 2009.

It is constructed using a waterproof, metal casing and has a curved, tempered glass face. It is 13.9 mm thick. The touchscreen is 1.43-inches (3.63cm) across, 352 x 288 pixels, and uses LG's Flash interface.

The LG-GD910 is compatible with 7.2 Mbit/s 3G HSDPA, which enables the high speed data transmission required to make video calls using the in-built camera. It also supports Bluetooth headsets, including stereo audio, and has a built-in speaker. There is a Text to Speech option for handling text messages and other information, and voice recognition features can be used to look up contact details and make calls.

The LG-GD910 will be available in Europe at the end of 2009 via the Orange network..It was launched in India in april 2010.

External links

- LG's official webpage for the GD910 [1]
- Engadget: LG's GD910 wrist phone in action [2]
- PocketPicks: Photo gallery from Mobile World Congress 2009 [3]

LG GD900

LG GD900

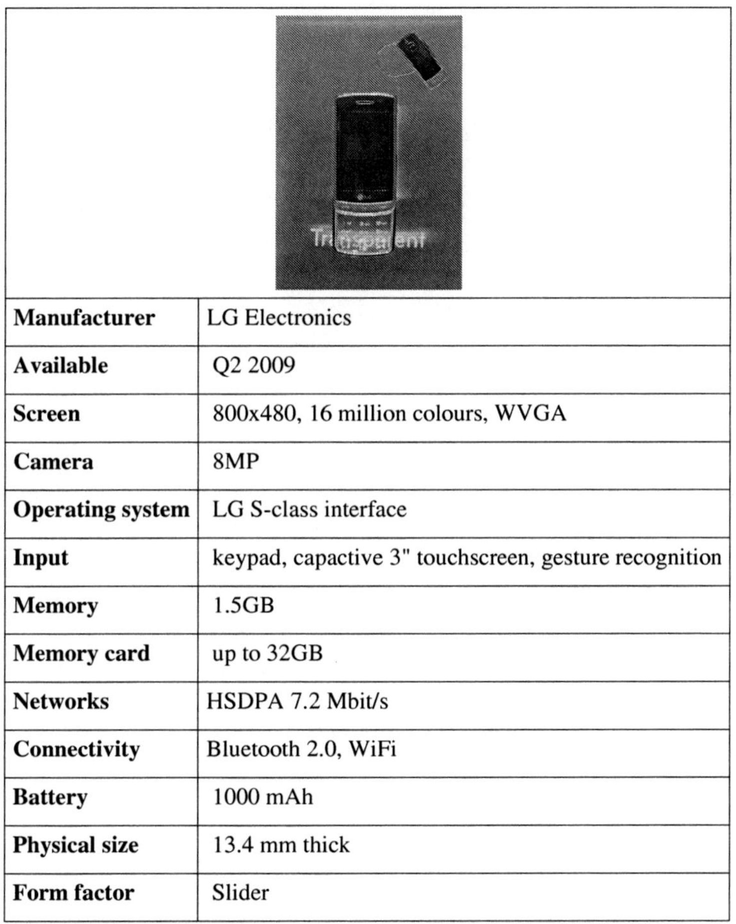

Manufacturer	LG Electronics
Available	Q2 2009
Screen	800x480, 16 million colours, WVGA
Camera	8MP
Operating system	LG S-class interface
Input	keypad, capactive 3" touchscreen, gesture recognition
Memory	1.5GB
Memory card	up to 32GB
Networks	HSDPA 7.2 Mbit/s
Connectivity	Bluetooth 2.0, WiFi
Battery	1000 mAh
Physical size	13.4 mm thick
Form factor	Slider

The **LG-GD900** is a fashion-focused slider with high end specifications phone from LG Electronics that was publicly unveiled at Mobile World Congress 2009. It is claimed to be the world's first transparent design phone. It comes with a dedicated Bluetooth headset that is also transparent in parts.

The transparent part of the GD900 is the sliding keypad, which is designed to glow when in operation. The main casing material is metal and the phone is 13.4mm thick.LG decided to ship GD900 with a tempered glass keypad like a screen.

In terms of features, the phone supports 7.2 Mbit/s HSDPA and has a rear-mounted 8MP camera with flash. LG released most of the phone's specification at the launch event in London on 28 May 2009. The GD900 was released in mid-June in Germany, and in 40 other countries worldwide on 1 July 2009.

External links

- Official LG press release [1]
- GD900 photo gallery from MWC09 [2]

LG KM900 (Arena)

LG KM900 (Arena)

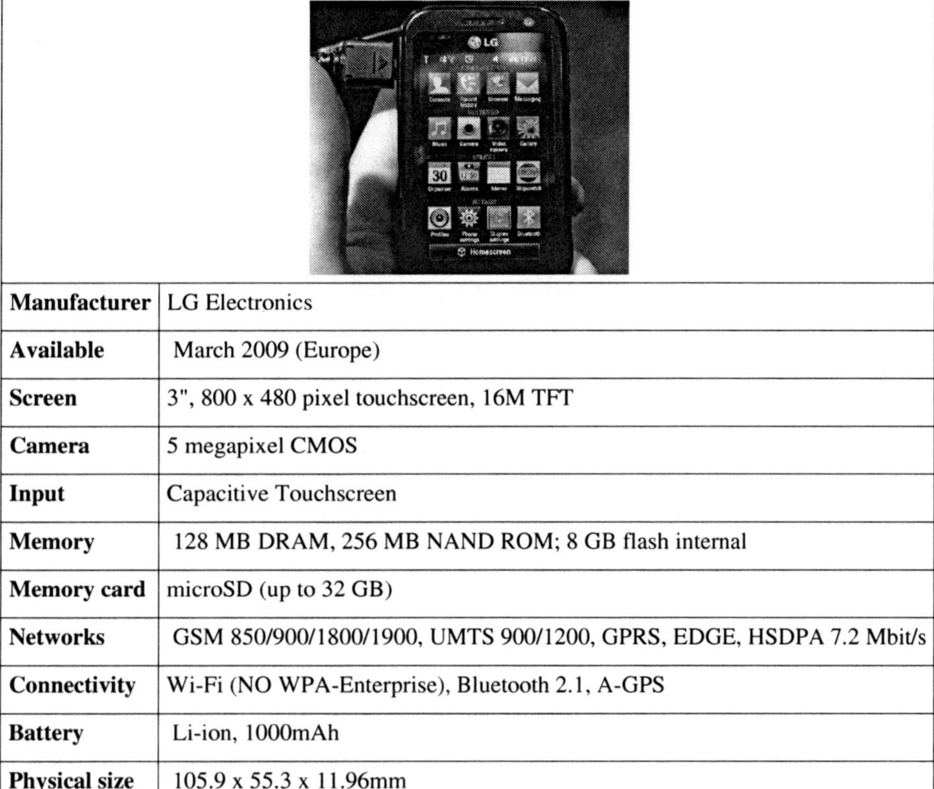

Manufacturer	LG Electronics
Available	March 2009 (Europe)
Screen	3", 800 x 480 pixel touchscreen, 16M TFT
Camera	5 megapixel CMOS
Input	Capacitive Touchscreen
Memory	128 MB DRAM, 256 MB NAND ROM; 8 GB flash internal
Memory card	microSD (up to 32 GB)
Networks	GSM 850/900/1800/1900, UMTS 900/1200, GPRS, EDGE, HSDPA 7.2 Mbit/s
Connectivity	Wi-Fi (NO WPA-Enterprise), Bluetooth 2.1, A-GPS
Battery	Li-ion, 1000mAh
Physical size	105.9 x 55.3 x 11.96mm
Weight	105g
Form factor	Candybar

The **LG-KM900**, or **LG Arena**, is an LG Electronics flagship multimedia phone for Q1 2009, succeeded by the LG GD900. Announced at the Mobile World Congress on February 16, 2009, the KM900 is the first phone to feature LG's new 3D S-Class user interface.

The S-Class is a capacitive touch-based 3D UI that lays out menus as if they were on a film reel, enabling you to drag your finger across the reels to scroll through the available options. It is based around a cube layout that provides four home screens that can be customised with different shortcuts. The UI reacts to the orientation of the Arena, switching between portrait and landscape modes.

Arena is a metal-cased device, available in silver, black Titanium & pink colour schemes. It has a 3-inch WVGA tempered glass multi-touch capable touchscreen with a resolution of 800 x 480 pixels.

The 5-Megapixel CMOS Schneider Kreuznach camera with LED flash can record QVGA video at up to 120 frames per second, DVD resolution (720x480) at 30 frames per second or encode H.264 at 15 frames per second. It has both automatic and manual focus options.

The phone has a built in web browser, with HSDPA (7.2 Mbit/s connection) and Wi-Fi capabilities (no WPA-Enterprise). The phone also features multi-touch zooming.

Arena is the first globally released phone to feature Dolby Mobile surround sound. Its FM transmitter can wirelessly feed into car or home stereo systems. Internal memory consists of 8 GB and there is a microSD slot that supports up to a further 32 GB.

Although the device is compatible with both Wi-Fi and YouTube, streaming YouTube videos using a wireless network is **not possible** with most firmware versions, including the newest ones. Some alternative (and older) firmware versions, like *VOO_02*, implement the solution for this problem, but were not developed by LG and result on device's performance decrease. In September 2009 the *V10P_00* version was released and updated the Google Maps version to 2.3.2, as well as some GPS functions, making possible for the handset to find your location in under 5 seconds. In older firmware version this would normally take more than 1 minute.

The most user stable and friendly firmware at present is the V10P_00 and V10F_00 which are both open and not locked to any firmware version, it is now possible to unlock [1] the handset to use on any network. Owners of the handset have modded and edited the V10P_00 to allow a windows theme [2] version of the firmware which is impressive. However, this phone has proven to be very unreliable with a constant tendency to freeze when you are multi-tasking or try to read a message too quickly after reception.

External links

- Official LG Arena website [3]
- Largest LG Arena Fan Forum [4]
- Engadget: video footage of the S-Class UI [5]

KF510

KF510

The **LG KF510** is a GSM mobile phone from LG Electronics which debuted in the 1st quarter of 2008. Measuring 11mm (.43"), the KF510 sports a metal frame and tempered glass display.

Specifications

LG KF510 mobile phone

Design Dimension: 104.5 x 49.5 x 10.9 mm

Main Display: 2.2" QVGA, 240x320 pixels

Audio

Camera features 3 MP, autofocus, flash

Messaging/SMS, EMS, MMS, Email

Java 2.0

WAP 2.0

Memory card slot/microSD

Call Records

Bluetooth TM

WLAN/Wi-Fi

USB

Data cable support

Browser

Vibration

Ringtones/Polyphonic

Radio /FM Radio

MP3 Player

Audio playback formats

Integrated speakers

HF speakerphone

Battery

Talk time

Standby time

Navigation

LG CT810 Incite

LG CT810 Incite

Manufacturer	LG Electronics
Carrier	AT&T (GSM) KT as LG-KU2000 SK Tel. as LG-SU200
Available	November 2008 for AT&T February 2009 (for both SK and KT)
Screen	240x400 px, 3.0 in (76 mm), 262K, 18-bit color LCD
Camera	3.2 megapixel AF back
Operating system	Windows Mobile 6.1 Professional
Input	Touchscreen
CPU	Qualcomm MSM7201A ARM Processor at 528 MHz
Default ringtone	AAC, AAC+, eAAC, eAAC+, MP3, WAV, WMA, Note: Have to use registry mod to be able to use ringtones over 600 KB.

The **LG Incite** is an Internet-enabled Windows Mobile Pocket PC smartphone designed and marketed by LG of Korea.

This phone has a reflective screen like the LG Shine but the difference is the chrome coated plastic

Product Details

Hardware

- Display : 3" Touch screen
  - Resolution (pixels) : 240 x 400 wQVGA display
  - Colors : 262K
- Keyboard : Touchscreen QWERTY On Screen, LG-Key On Screen
- Camera : 3.2MP Resolution, Live video capture and playback is also supported

Software

- Operating System : Windows Mobile 6.1 Professional
  - Windows Media Player Mobile 10 Installed
    - Supported music formats : MP3 +AAC + eAAC+. EAAC+ WMA, WAV
- Streaming Radio
  - XM Satellite Radio, Pandora(for CT810, excluded in KU and SU series)
  - Built-in FM Radio with RDS
- SMS and MMS Service : Available to send Pictures and Videos.
- Mobile Email
  - Microsoft Direct Push
- Web browser
- Built-in Calendar, Alarm clock, Call Waiting, Caller ID, Personal Organizer(LG Today Application)
- Address book
- Call Forwarding
- Multitasking
- Use voice and data simultaneously

Carrier Supports

AT&T

- AT&T Mobile Music
- MusicID - Identify songs you're listening to
- Instant Messaging (IM) that supports AOL, Yahoo!, & Windows Live Messenger
- Xpress Mail - access work and personal email, including Microsoft Outlook, Lotus Notes, Yahoo! Mail, AOL, Windows Live and more
- MEdia(TM) Net for wireless internet access
- CV - news, sports, weather, entertainment and more

- MEdia(TM) Mall

SK Telecom

- SK Telecom Total Message Service Application(kr:통합메세지함)
- Nate(include mPlayOn) : WIPI - A Java-like VM for Most Korean Handheld Device
- MySmart : SK Telecom's Mobile AppStore
- Sync Mail : Push Mail Application

KT

- SHOW(include SHOW Download Pack) : Like Nate, This app is also WIPI VM.
- WebSurfing : Pull style Web Browser

Technical specifications

Battery

- Battery Type : 1300 mAh Lithium-ion polymer
- Talk time : Up to 8.7 hours
- Standby time : 21 days

Dimensions

- Weight : 4.23 ounces
- Size (inches) : 4.21 x 2.2 x 0.55 inches
- (millimeters) : 106.9 x 55.88 x 13.97mm

Memory

- Internal memory storage : 256 MB ROM, 128 MB RAM
- Expandable memory storage : 32 GB
- Memory format : microSD(TM)

Support Connection

- Wi-Fi IEEE 802.11 b/g
- 3G UMTS/HSDPA Tri-Band(850/1900/2100Mhz)
- GSM Quad-band(850/900/1800/1900Mhz) with EDGE(High Speed Data Network)
- Bluetooth (Version 2.0 with EDR)
- Micro USB
- (for Only CT-810) Qualcomm A-GPS

External links

- LG Incite Main Page [1]
- LG Incite Updates [2]
- LG Incite Blog(Korean) [3]
- AT&T's Incite Page [4]
- KT(SHOW)'s Incite Page [5]

LG KF600

LG KF600

The **LG KF600** is a GSM mobile phone manufactured by LG, released in March 2008. It features an 'Interact Pad', a touch sensitive pad below the screen which changes to suit the activity currently being done on the phone.

Specifications

- Dimensions - 101.2 x 50.7 x 14.1 mm
- Weight - 107 g
- Display Type - TFT, 256K colors
- Screen Size - 240 x 320 pixels, 2.0 inches
- Touch-sensitive lower display - 256K colors TFT, 176 x 240 pixels, 1.49 inches

LG KG290

LG KG290

The **KG 290** Rhino is a mobile telephone manufactured by LG. It is a slide form phone with a mainly plastic body and comes in black or silver. It has a 1.3 megapixel camera and Bluetooth. Other features include GPRS connection, calendar, memos and picture and video capture. It also has a 1.77 inch screen and a micro SD card slot although it does not support micro SDHC cards. The battery lasts up to 200 hours on standby and 2 hours talk time.

LG enV Touch (VX11000)

LG enV Touch (VX11000)

Manufacturer	LG Electronics
Carrier	Verizon Wireless
Available	June 5, 2009
Screen	LCD 800 x 480
Exterior screen	LCD 800 x 480
Camera	3.2 megapixel
Operating system	BREW
Memory	250 MB
Memory card	up to 16 GB (microSD)
Networks	EVDO, 1X
Connectivity	Bluetooth / Micro USB Cable / 3.5mm Audio Jack
Battery	950 mAh
Physical size	4.52 x 2.16 x 0.66 inches (115 x 55 x 17 mm)
Weight	140g (4.92 oz)
Form factor	Clamshell (Candybar/flip)
Predecessor	LG Voyager (VX10000)
Hearing aid compatibility	M4/T4

The **LG enV Touch** also known as the **Voyager 2, or VX11000** is an internet-enabled, multimedia device created by LG Electronics for use with Verizon Wireless. The phone was released on June 5, 2009 as a successor to the LG Voyager. The phone's external screen is touch enabled with a virtual keyboard and buttons. The internal screen features a QWERTY keyboard and both screens have a WVGA resolution. The phone's functions include a 3.2 megapixel camera with flash, a portable media player, text messaging, e-mail support, a web browser, a built-in accelerometer, and Verizon's GPS navigation software, VZ Navigator. It is a dual-band CDMA phone using EVDO for data communications.

Features

The enV Touch has a larger external touch screen and internal screen display than its predecessor, the Voyager, as well as a camera with a newer 3.2 megapixel lens, an LED flash, and stronger vibration. The QWERTY keyboard retained a similar size to the original Voyager's but its layout was altered slightly to move the space key to the middle of the keyboard, unlike previous enV devices which had the key on the both sides of the layout.

The enV Touch includes text messaging and web browsing capabilities, as well as camera and video recording, voice commands, and speaker phone. The phone supports Verizon's VCast Video/Music, Visual Voicemail, and VZ Navigator services. However, the phone lacks the VCast Mobile T.V. support of the original Voyager. It features accelerometer motion sensors similar to those found in iPhone-based devices for games such as Need for Speed. The enV Touch also features a Document Viewer that can display Microsoft Excel, PowerPoint, and Word documents, as well as PDF documents. The most recent software revision is version 9, which includes a new Internet Browser, although new updates are released periodically.

References

http://reviews.cnet.com/cell-phones/lg-env-touch-verizon/1805-6454_7-33665903.html

External links

- LG enV Touch Updates [1]
- *us.lge*: enV Touch [2]
- *us.lge*: Datasheet [3]

LG Rumor 2

LG Rumor 2

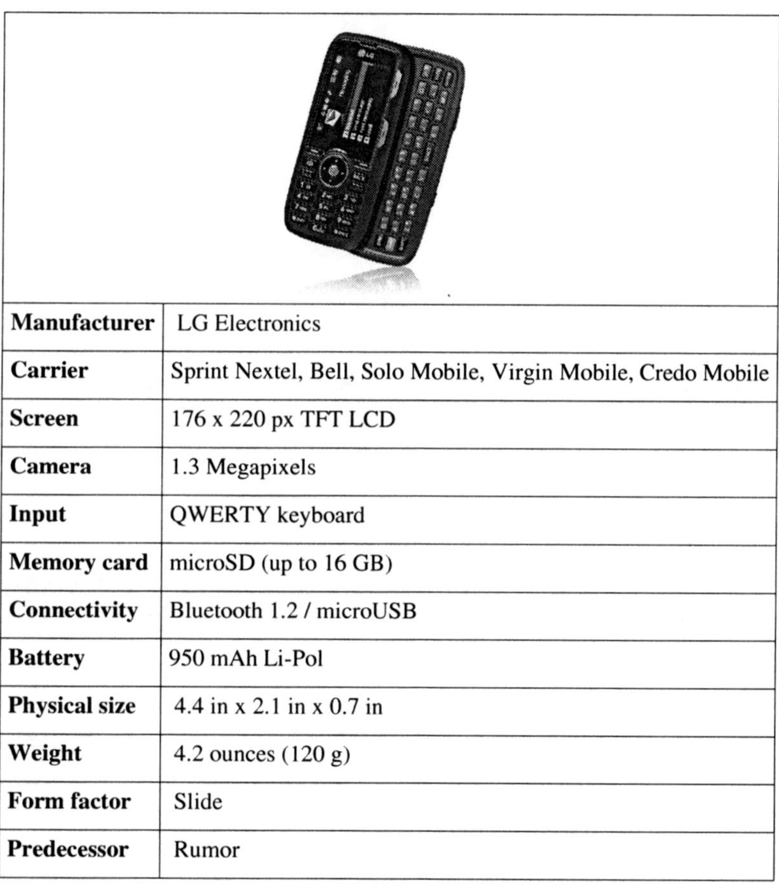

Manufacturer	LG Electronics
Carrier	Sprint Nextel, Bell, Solo Mobile, Virgin Mobile, Credo Mobile
Screen	176 x 220 px TFT LCD
Camera	1.3 Megapixels
Input	QWERTY keyboard
Memory card	microSD (up to 16 GB)
Connectivity	Bluetooth 1.2 / microUSB
Battery	950 mAh Li-Pol
Physical size	4.4 in x 2.1 in x 0.7 in
Weight	4.2 ounces (120 g)
Form factor	Slide
Predecessor	Rumor

The **LG Rumor 2** (**LG Rumour2** and **LG Rumeur2** in Canada) is a Sprint Nextel, Bell Mobility, Solo Mobile, Virgin Mobile USA and Virgin Mobile Canada messaging phone manufactured by LG Electronics. It is available in black titanium, vibrant blue, and orange. The phones are offered by Sprint in Black, Blue, and Orange and were released in March 2009. The regular price of the phone is $249.99.

It is the follow up of the LG Rumor (LX260) that came out in September 2007. The Rumor 2 has been updated from the original version. Although it is a bit bigger and slightly heavier, the QWERTY keyboard has been adjusted to have 4 full lines of the keyboard enabling more space for texting. The front keys have been polished to make what the critics say a glossier and more stylish look. Unlike the original Rumor, the LG Rumor 2 does not have video recording capabilities. It is suspected by the internet community that this was to prevent a loophole where customers could create a blank video with music on their computers and assign them as ring tones, thereby subverting any subscription or download fees.

Features

Main Features

Like the original Rumor, the Rumor 2 has many features including a slide-out QWERTY Keyboard in addition to the standard 12-button keypad, a 1.3 megapixel camera, and a 320x240 pixel screen. The QWERTY keyboard easily slides out from the right. The screen rotates as the keyboard opens up.

Special Features

The digital camera does not have an LED flash, but does include black and white, negative, and sepia color tones as well as various fun frames. It is very similar to the original Rumor camera. There is a self-timer, night mode functions/ brightness, and white balance controls (as mentioned above). The Rumor 2 is Bluetooth-compatible, supports MP3 music formats and Sprint Navigation (Sprint's map service).

Virgin Mobile Additions

Virgin Mobile added Ultimate Inbox to the LG Rumor 2 which includes several choices of push E-mail communication with support for Yahoo! Mail, Windows Live Hotmail, AOL Mail, Gmail, and an additional user-defined POP or IMAP account. There is also instant messaging support for AOL Instant Messenger, Yahoo! Messenger, Google Talk, and Windows Live Messenger. According to the devices about screen the functionality is powered by MFluent. The LG Rumor 2 for Virgin Mobile is currently only available in black/silver/blue. Other additions to the phone include Virgin Mobile UI and VM default wallpapers and ringtones.

Storage

The phone can hold up to 600 contacts with additional numbers, notes, and email addresses. The phone supports up to 16GB of storage via the MicroSD port on the right side of the phone.

Keyboard

The QWERTY keyboard on the Rumor 2 is vital to the selling of the phone. The keyboard has 4 rows of keys. The number keys now have their own row, as opposed to the old keyboard where they had to share a row on the top. The keys are still made with rubber. Unlike the original Rumor, the improved keyboard includes arrow keys for easier navigation and the "enter" and "back" button.

Entertainment

The Rumor 2 offers many different sources of entertainment. From the Sprint website, there are 101 games to pick from with different prices. Messaging is the main source of entertainment from the phone. The Rumor 2 is known for its convenient messaging. The Rumor 2 also allows mobile email. Any email domain is allowed for access. The music player on the phone cant hold up to 4,000 songs using the MicroSD chip..

Specifications

Type	Specification
Weight	4.2 oz
Dimensions	4.4" x 2.1" x 0.7"
Form Factor	Slide
Talk Time	5.5 hours
Display	Type: LCD (Color TFT/TFD), 10 line, Colors: 262,144, Size: 176 x 220 pixels
Memory	Phone internal: 16384KB, Additional MicroSD memory (up to 16 GB)
Phone Book Capacity	600
GPS / Location	Yes, enabled by default. Note: GPS does NOT work with Google Maps on Virgin Mobile.
Digital TTY/TDD	Yes
Hearing Aid Compatible	Rating: M3
Multiple Languages	English, Spanish, French
Vibrate	Yes
Bluetooth †	Supported Profiles: A2DP, AVRCP, GAVDP, HFP, HFP 1.5, PBAP, HSP, HID (keyboard only), BPP, FTP, GOEP, SDAP/SDP, DUN, OPP, SPP, Stereo Streaming, AVDTP, OBEX
Multiple Numbers per Name	Yes
Picture ID	Yes
Ringer ID	Yes, and text message ID
Voice Dialing	No (Voice Control Available)
Custom Graphics	Yes
Custom Ringtones	Yes

Data-Capable	Yes
Flight Mode	Yes
Packet Data	Technology: 1xRTT
WAP / Web Browser	Yes, dial up and USB tethered
Predictive Text Entry	Technology: T9 Predictive / QWERTY Word Prediction
Side Keys	Left side: Volume, Camera
Memory Card Slot	Card Type: MicroSD up to 16GB
MMS	Yes
Text Messaging	Yes, up to 160 characters (per message portion [delivered as different text messages], 6 portion maximum per message), 25 recipients at a time
Music Player	Yes, Supported Formats: MP3, AAC, AAC+, M4A, MID
Camera	Resolution: 1.3 Megapixels
Video Capture	No
Alarm	Yes
Calculator	Basic
Calendar	Yes
Voice Memo	Yes, ability to record memo and calls
BREW	No
Games	Yes
Unit Converter	Yes

† For Virgin Mobile, Bluetooth profiles are restricted to HSP, HFP, A2DP, AVRCP.

Availability

Popularity

The Rumor 2 is slowly becoming more popular after Sprint announced the Rumor would no longer be sold with their plan.

The LG Rumor 2 was also featured in the music video of 'Telephone' performed by Lady Gaga

Colors

So far, the only companies that offer the Rumor 2 are Sprint Nextel, Bell Mobility, Solo Mobile and Virgin Mobile. There are 4 available colors (Black Titanium, Vibrant Blue, Green[6], and Orange).

LG Rumor Touch

In early 2010 LG & Sprint offered a new, updated version of the Rumor2 called the LG Rumor Touch with a five-row QWERTY keyboard, instead of a three-row for Rumor or a four-row for Rumor2. It also includes a touch screen. It is currently offered at $29.99 with a two year contract from Sprint. The Rumor Touch does include video recording capabilities that the Rumor has, but the Rumor2 did not include.

The phone is available through Virgin Mobile at $149.99 and does have GPS support in Google Maps.

References

- http://www.bell.ca/shopping/en_CA_ON.LG-Rumour-2/97881.details?contractId=prepaid

LG Lotus (LX600)

LG Lotus (LX600)

The Lotus on the Sprint Nextel network	
Manufacturer	LG Electronics
Carrier	Sprint Nextel
Available	North America
Screen	2.4"
Exterior screen	1.3"
Connectivity	USB & Bluetooth
Battery	900 mAh Li-Ion
Physical size	3.30" (H) x 2.40" (W) x 0.70" (D)
Weight	3.7 oz
Form factor	Clamshell

LG Lotus (**LX600**) is a phone Introduced in September 10, 2008. The phone is marketed as a fashion forward device by Sprint Nextel. It was designed by fashion designer Christian V. Siriano.

The LG Lotus has enhanced messaging features including a wide display screen and a full QWERTY keyboard. It is available exclusively through Sprint.:

Features

- QWERTY Keyboard
- External Music Controls
- 2.0 Megapixel Camera & Camcorder
- Bluetooth Capable
- microSDTM Memory Port

A scarf was also designed by Siriano to complement the phone. The scarf features a pocket specifically tailored to fit the LG Lotus.

External links

- Official LG Lotus website [1]

LG Xenon

LG Xenon

Manufacturer	LG Electronics
Screen	240 x 400 pixels 262k colors
Exterior screen	2.8 inches
Camera	2.0 megapixels Flash
Operating system	Symbian S60
Default ringtone	MP3
Memory card	microSD card (holds up to a 16gb)
Networks	UMTS / HSDPA / EDGE / GPRS GSM 850 / 900 / 1800 / 1900
Battery	950 mAh 4 hours talk time 11 days stand by
Physical size	4.16 x 2.11 x 0.62 inches
Weight	3.81 ounces (108 g)
Form factor	Slider, Touch

The LG Xenon (LG GR500) is a mobile phone manufactured by LG Electronics, which features a touch screen and QWERTY keyboard on AT&T's 3G network. It offers a flash for the 2.0 mega pixel camera, GPS, multi tasking, a menu or favorite contacts, and a microSD slot for music, pictures, and video. Voice dialing and video share are among the features on this phone. However, contrary to popular belief on many articles, the LG Xenon lacks Wi-Fi capability. It also has photo editing.

Design

The LG Xenon comes in three colors; Black, Blue, Red, and Purple. It runs on an OS similar to its predecessor the Lg Vu, and has a slide out QWERTY and resistive touch screen. Its keyboard has dedicated buttons (@, .com, New Text Message, Mobile Email, Address Book, Instant Messaging (AIM, Windows Live and Yahoo!) and MEdia Net) for prompt text and email messages. When opened, the phone is viewed in a wider aspect than when closed. A lock / unlock button on the right side allows the phone to be used while it is not open. The default themes are white with blue outlining, and black with red outlining.

See also

- List of LG mobile phones
- LG Electronics
- LG Shine
- LG Vu
- AT&T
- Samsung Eternity, a competitor.
- Samsung Impression, a competitor.

LG enV3 (VX9200)

LG enV3 (VX9200)

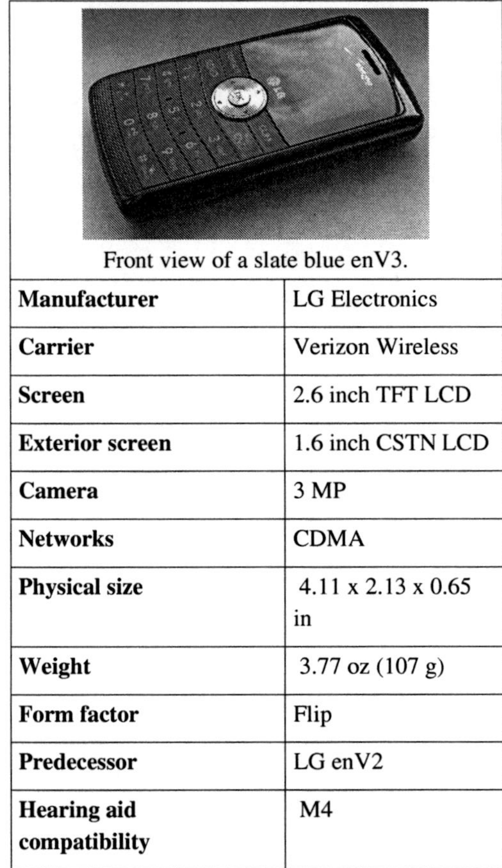

Front view of a slate blue enV3.

Manufacturer	LG Electronics
Carrier	Verizon Wireless
Screen	2.6 inch TFT LCD
Exterior screen	1.6 inch CSTN LCD
Camera	3 MP
Networks	CDMA
Physical size	4.11 x 2.13 x 0.65 in
Weight	3.77 oz (107 g)
Form factor	Flip
Predecessor	LG enV2
Hearing aid compatibility	M4

The **LG enV3** is a mobile phone built by LG Electronics, and released from Verizon Wireless in the United States and Telus Mobility in Canada (as the **Keybo 2**). It succeeded the LG enV2. Along with a slimmer design, the enV3 also boasts a full keyboard, a 2.6 inch screen and a 3.0 Megapixel camera. In addition to standard phone and text messaging capabilities, the enV3 can be used as a portable music player as well as Internet capabilities such as e-mail and web browsing. The phone is also Bluetooth enabled.

Design

The enV3 phone has a slimmer design than its previous version. It has a circular D-pad on the front, a number keypad, and a slightly larger external display than the enV2. Along with the number keypad, there is a dedicated Contacts button, a Clear button and the Send and End/Power keys. Once it's opened, the enV3 has a larger 2.6-inch main display and a full QWERTY keyboard. There is a Favorites button for accessing the set favorite contacts and a dedicated text messaging button, which opens a blank text message. The navigation array on the right of the keyboard consists of the typical Send and End/Power keys, a four-way square toggle, a middle OK key, a Clear key, and a dedicated speakerphone key. On the left side of the phone is the camera button and volume adjuster. On the right side, there is a microSD memory card slot and a 2.5mm headset jack. The charger jack is on the bottom of the phone and the camera lens is on the back, as is an LED flash.

It comes in two colors - slate blue and maroon.

Features

The enV3 has a number of improvements over its previous versions. Starting with the very basics, the phone has an 1,000-entry phone book with room in each entry for five numbers, two e-mail addresses and a street address. Other features include voice commands and dialing, calendar, alarm clock, world clock, notepad, mobile instant messenger (AIM, Windows Live Messenger, and Yahoo), tip calculator, and Bluetooth. Another feature is the ability to add a social network e-mail address in the "Blogs" section of the Messaging menu, allowing someone to update their photos or videos to Facebook or MySpace.

For advanced users, there is a large USB mass storage, GPS with VZ Navigator support, e-mail and visual voice mail. There's also Dashboard with Mobile Web, which a Web portal that leads to Web channels and information sources such as ESPN, weather channels, entertainment, news, and most importantly, a shortcut to a full HTML Web browser.

The enV3's camera is a 3.0-Megapixel camera. With the new camera, the user is able to take pictures in six different resolutions, five white balance presets and five color effects. There are also four special shot modes: Smile shot, which automatically takes a picture when a person smiles; Panorama, which stitches together three photos shot from left to right; Intelligent shot, which automatically adjusts the white balance and color saturation based on the environment, and Dual Display mode, which turns on the external display, allowing self-portraits.

The env3 has a wide range of music services, like V Cast Music, where the user can download songs over the air, the V Cast Music with Rhapsody service, where a person can purchase and download songs directly to the phone for $1.99; it can also play non-protected music files from an SD memory card, along with download songs straight from a computer using a USB cable. The enV3 also has the capability of using Verizon's Song ID, which can listen to a sample of a song and return the title and artist.

Defects in early versions

Many env3 users have complained about the device repeatedly powering down on its own, even after installing firmware updates. This has been officially attributed to a physical defect in early versions of the phone causing the battery contacts to be pulled away from the phone when even slight pressure is applied to the phone. Verizon will replace these phones at no charge.

Available accessories

Accessories endorsed by Verizon Wireless include Bluetooth headsets and headphones, microSD cards and adapters as well as certain brands of speakers. There are also a number of different cases, which come in multitudes of different colors and patterns. Covers and screen protectors are also widely popular.

External links

- CNET Review [1]
- CNET News | "LG enV3 is small but impressive" [2]
- Phone Arena [3]
- LG enV3 VX9200 Phone (Verizon Wireless) [4]

LG Prada II (KF900)

LG Prada II (KF900)

Manufacturer	LG Electronics
Screen	256K colour TFT touchscreen, 240 x 400 px
Camera	5 megapixel with auto-focus and flash, plus front facing camera
Memory	microSD Internal Memory Slot
Networks	GSM, EDGE, UMTS, HSDPA
Connectivity	Bluetooth 2.1, USB 2.0, WiFi
Physical size	104.4×54×16.75 mm
Weight	130 g
Form factor	Candybar/Slide

The **LG KF900**, also known as the **LG Prada II**, is a touchscreen, with slide out qwerty keyboard, mobile phone made by LG Electronics. It is the second version of the Prada phone, following the original LG Prada (KE850). The phone's looks are basically the same as the original Prada, but the Prada II is slightly thicker, taller and heavier, to support a slide-out full QWERTY keyboard. There is also a front-facing camera for use with video calling. The interface has been updated from the original. The camera has been increased from 2 to 5 megapixels with a LED photolight. The Prada II also now supports 3G and HSPDA for faster internet browsing. The Prada II has support for the Prada Link, which is bluetooth watch that allows information on incoming phone calls or text messages, the phone's alarm, or the world time clock.

Features

- Capacitive, Multi-touch Touch Screen
- Music Player (MP3, AAC, AAC+, WMA, RA)
- Multitasking
- Video Player (MPEG4, H.263, H.264)
- Active flash UI
- Document Viewer (ppt, doc, xls, pdf, txt)
- Accelerometer

- Full QWERTY keyboard

Specifications

General

- Form Factor: Touchscreen with slide-out qwerty keyboard
- Dimensions: 104.4×54×16.75 mm
- Weight: 130 g
- Main Screen Type: TFT mutli-touch touchscreen, 256K colors
- Main Screen Size/Resolution: 240 x 400 pixels, 3 inches
- Messaging: SMS, EMS, MMS, Email
- Operating System: Flash UI
- Built-in Hands-free: Yes
- Voice-dial/memo: Yes
- Vibration: Yes
- Organizer: Yes
- Office Document Viewer: .ppt, .doc, .xls, .pdf, .txt
- Battery Stand-By: Up to 400 h
- Battery Talk Time: Up to 3 h

Connectivity

- 3G Network: GSM 900 / 1800 / 1900
- HSDPA: 7.2 Mbps
- Blue-tooth: Yes, v2.0 with A2DP
- USB: Yes, v2.0
- WiFi

Multimedia

- 5MP camera: 5 MP, 2592x1944 pixels, with Schneider-Kreuznach certified lens
- Front facing camera: used for video calling
- Internal Memory: 60 MB shared memory
- Memory Slot: microSD (TransFlash), up to 8GB
- Music: MP3, WAV, WMA,MIDI, AAC, AAC+, eAAC+, RA, AMR-NB
- Video: MPEG4, H.263, H.264, 3GP, RV
- Radio: Yes
- Ringtones: Polyphonic (40 channels), MP3
- Speakers: Built-in handsfree

Latest Software Version: V10P (download located here: http://www.lge.com/uk/support/product/support-product-profile-mobile-redux. jsp?customerModelCode=KF900& initialTab=documents&

targetPage=support-product-profile)

See also

- LG Prada (KE850)

External links

- LG KF900 - LG Electronics [1]
- Official Phone Website [7]

LG Viewty Smart

LG Viewty Smart

The **LG-GC900** (known and marketed as the **LG Viewty Smart**) is a mobile phone manufactured by LG Electronics. It was released in June 2009 as successor to the LG Viewty (KU990).

Manufacturer	LG Electronics
Available	2009
Screen	TFT, touchscreen, 3", 480x800 (WQVGA)
Camera	8.0 megapixel, video 30 frame/s or slow-motion video 120 frame/s, Strobe Flash
Second camera	VGA Video call (Front)
Memory	1.5 GB
Memory card	MicroSD
Networks	HSDPA, GSM, GPRS
Connectivity	Bluetooth 1.2, USB 2.0, Wi-Fi
Physical size	56.1 x 108.9 x 12.4 (W x L x D)
Weight	102 grams
Form factor	Candybar

LG Versa

LG Versa

Manufacturer	LG Electronics
Carrier	Verizon, Telus
Available	September 9, 2009
Screen	LCD 240 x 480
Camera	2.0 megapixel
Operating system	BREW
Memory	310 MB
Memory card	up to 16 GB (microSD)
Networks	EVDO, 1XRTT
Connectivity	Bluetooth / Micro USB Cable / 2.5mm Audio Jack
Battery	Li – Ion, 1100 mAH
Physical size	4.16 x 2.07 x 0.54 inches
Weight	140g (4.92 oz)
Form factor	Clamshell (Candybar/flip)
Hearing aid compatibility	M4/T4

Features

- **Network**
  - Type: CDMA Dual Band (800 / 1900 MHz)
  - Data: CDMA 2000 1xRTT / 1xEV-DO Rev.0 / 1xEV-DO Rev.A
  - 3G Capable: Yes
- **Size**
  - Dimensions: 4.16 x 2.07 x 0.54 inches
  - Weight: 3.81 oz
- **Battery**

- Type: Li – Ion, 1100 mAH
- Talk: 4.83 Hours (290 Minutes)
- Standby: 430 Hours (18 Days)

- **Main Display**
  - Resolution: 240 x 480 Pixels
  - Type: 262,144 TFT
  - Physical Size: 3.00 Inches
  - Features: Light Sensor
  - Touch Screen: Yes With Hand Writing Recognition
- **Additional Display**
  - Resolution: 120 x 56 Pixels
  - Type: Monochrome OLED
  - Features: Only Available On The QWERTY Keypad Attachment
- **Camera**
  - Resolution: 2.0 Megapixels
  - Video Capture: Yes
  - Features: Auto focus, Flash (LED), Digital Zoom, White balance, Effects, Panorama
- **Multimedia**
  - Video Playback: MPEG 4, 3GP, 3GP2, WMV
  - Music Player: MP3, AAC, ACC+, WMA
- **Memory**
  - Memory Slot: Micro SD/Micro SDHC
  - Built In: 310 MB
- **Input**
  - Keypad: Detachable
- **Connectivity**
  - USB: Micro USB
  - Bluetooth: Version 2.1, Stereo Bluetooth
  - Connectors: Headset Jack (2.5mm)

External links

- LG Versa Review [1]
- LG Versa Phonescoop [2]
- LG Versa Forum [3]

GW525

GW525

[[Image:  An LG GW525 Closed 250px	
Manufacturer	LG Electronics
Carrier	Allphones, Optus, Telechoice
Available	Q4 2009
Screen	2.8" Touchscreen
Camera	Yes
Operating system	S-Class
Input	QWERTY Keypad and Touchscreen
Memory	40MB
Memory card	8GB MicroSD
Networks	GSM 850/900/1800/1900, UMTS 900/2100/HSPDA Speed 7.2Mpbs
Connectivity	Bluetooth, USB 2.0 Cable
Battery	950mAh Li-Ion
Physical size	106.5 x 53 x 15.9 mm

Weight	125.5g
Form factor	Slider

The "GW525" is a mobile phone manufactured by LG Electronics. The phone is designed to be low cost, but compared to its main competitors, it is actually relatively expensive.

Main Features

The LG GW525 is a basic slider phone. The key features are:

- QWERTY keypad
- 2.8" Touch Screen
- Accelerometer
- 3 Megapixel camera
- WAP
- Video Calling
- Speaker Phone (Handsfree)
- 2.0 Java Support
- In-built Games
- Customisable widgets
- Calendar and Organiser
- Alarm
- Customisable Wallpaper
- Downloadable Ringtones & Wallpapers

In The Box

When you buy the phone you should get:

- LG GW525 Mobile Phone
- LG Approved GW525 950mAh Li-Ion Battery
- A/C Charger
- USB Data Cable
- LG GW525 PC-Sync Software CD
- Handsfree

Technical Specifications

Here are the technical specifications of this phone.

Carrier Support

Theoretically, the phone should work on any network, if you unlock it. However, according to the phones website [1], the phone will work on All Phones, Optus and TeleChoice only.

Operating Frequency

GSM: 850/900/1500/1900
UMTS: 900/2100/HSPDA Speed 7.2Mbps

Dimensions

Height: 106.5mm
Width: 53mm
Thickness: 15.9mm
Weight: 125.5g

Screen

Size:2.8" Touch Screen
Colours: 262k
Pixels:240x400 (Width x Height)

Memory

Internal: 40 Megabytes
Expandable: Yes, up to 8 Gigabytes MicroSD **Phone Book:** Up to 1000 Entries

Messaging

The phone can send normal SMS text messages (with T9 (predictive text), as well as MMS, with Video MMS capabilities
E-Mail: POP3 and EAS

Camera

The phone has a 3 MegaPixel camera with 2 times digital zoom.

Media

Music: Audio formats include MP3, AAC, AAC+ and AAC++ **Video:** Video formats include H.263, H.264 and MPEG4 The phone also comes with a FM Radio, and like most other phones you need the headset that comes with the phone.

Battery

The battery that comes with the phone is 950mAh Li-Ion, with 400 hours of stand-by time and 4.5 hours of talk time.

Connectivity

The phone comes with Bluetooth and a USB 2.0 connector for PC-Sync.

See also

LG Electronics
LG Electronics Australia [2]

LG Chocolate (BL40)

LG Chocolate (BL40)

Manufacturer	LG
Screen	345x800 px (0.28 Megapixels) (21:9 aspect ratio), 4 inch, TFT LCD display, up to 16 million colours
Camera	5.0 megapixels f/2.8 Schneider KREUZNACH Tessar lens
Input	Touchscreen, Compact QWERTY (Two characters/key)
Memory	1.1Gb internal
Memory card	MicroSD up to 32Gb
Networks	HSDPA (3.5G), Quad band GSM / GPRS
Physical size	128 x 51 x 10.9 mm
Weight	129g
Form factor	candybar
Series	LG Chocolate

The **BL40** is a model of South Korean electronic brand LG's brand of LG Chocolate phones.

External links

- LG Chocolate BL40 [1]

LG VX5500

LG VX5500

The *LG VX55350* is an mobile phone used by Verizon Wireless. The phone was released on October 31, 2008 by LG. It is also used on Virgin Mobile. The phone contains the following features:

- VGA camera
- Bluetooth
- TYY capable
- keypad for quick dialing
- Front screen
- Media Center
- VZ Navigator
- Touch screen

Carriers

Verizon Wireless

AT&T

T-mobile

Cricket wireless

Specifications

- WAP/ Web Browser - Yes
- Text Messaging - Yes
- Picture Messaging - Yes
- Video Messaging - Yes
- Games - Yes
- Camera - VGA Camera
- Video Capture - Yes
- Voice Memo - Yes
- Application Download - Via Media Center
- Voicemail - Yes

External links

- LG Mobile Phones [1]
- Verizon Wireless [6]
- LG VX5500 on Verizon Wireless [1]

See also

- List of LG mobile phones
- Verizon Wireless
- LG Electronics
- LG VX8300

LG GW620

LG GW620

Manufacturer	LG Electronics
Type	Smartphone
Release date	November 2009
Operating system	Android 1.5
CPU	528 MHz
Display	320 x 480 px, 3.0 in
Input	Resistive touchscreen TFT, QWERTY keyboard
Camera	5.0 megapixel, auto focus, LED flash
Connectivity	microUSB 2.0, Bluetooth 2.0, Wi-Fi b/g, GPRS, EDGE, 3G
Dimensions	106 x 54.5 x 16 mm
Weight	139g

The **LG GW620 Eve**, also known as the **LG InTouch Max**, is a smartphone manufactured by LG Electronics. It is the first smartphone from LG that runs the Android operating system.

According to LG's managing director in Levant, Kevin Cha, "This Android phone is just one of many smartphone models we plan to introduce worldwide in the years ahead." In Canada, the LG GW620 is distributed by Rogers Wireless.

See also

- List of Android devices

External links

- www.lg-gw620.com [1], official website.
- LG GW620 at PDAdb.net [2]
- http://openetna.com/ [3] open firmware project

Vx8360

Vx8360

The **lg-vx8360** is the replacement for the LG VX8350. The phones are almost identical. It is marketed as a multimedia phone with a external music player and a 1.3 megapixel camera.

External links

- http://www.lge.com/us/mobile-phones/LG-VX8360.jsp
- http://reviews.cnet.com/cell-phones/lg-vx8360-verizon-wireless/4505-6454_7-33490611.html
- http://www.phonearena.com/htmls/LG-VX8360-phone-p_2966.html

LG eXpo

LG eXpo

Manufacturer	LG Electronics
Type	Slider phone
Release date	2009
Operating system	Windows Mobile 6.5
Power	Li-Po, 1500 mAh
CPU	Qualcomm, 1000 MHz
Storage capacity	microSD/microSDHC
Memory	256 MB RAM / 512 MB ROM
Display	Resistive screen, 480 x 800 pixels
Input	Stylus pen
Camera	5 Megapixel
Connectivity	HTML, WAP 2.0, USB, 802.11b/802.11g, Bluetooth
Dimensions	113 x 55 x 16 mm
Weight	147 grams / 5.20 oz

LG eXpo is a mobile phone designed for business users, and manufactured by LG Electronics. It runs Microsoft's Windows Mobile operating system, and was released in December, 2009.

The phone features a 3.2 inch resistive screen, which is operated by holding a stylus pen. The stylus is stored externally, in a cylindrical container with a cap. It is the first mobile phone to feature a handheld projector.

External links

- LG eXpo Official Site by AT&T [1]
- LG eXpo Picture [2]
- LG eXpo Press Release [3]
- LG eXpo Official Site [4]
- LG eXpo Review by Gizmodo [5]
- LG eXpo Forum [6]
- cnet review on LG eXpo [7]

LG CF360

LG CF360

The **LG CF360** is a cellular phone made by LG, and was sold basically for AT&T. It was released in December 2009, just before Christmas. Its is a basic slide up phone. In the addition to the phone being black with blue numbers and accents, the phone is also in black with red numbers and accents.

Features

- Media .NET
- Video Sharing
- Multimedia Messaging
- Mobile E-mail
- Camera Phone
- Bluetooth
- Mobile Games
- AT&T GPS
- 3G Speed
- Text Messaging
- Hands Free Speakerphone
- USB Connectivity .

LG GD510

LG GD510

Manufacturer	LG Electronics
Available	October 2009
Screen	256K colour TFT touchscreen, 240 × 400 px
Camera	3.15 megapixel, video QVGA (15FPS)
Memory	microSD Internal Memory Slot, adjacent to battery.
Networks	GSM/GPRS/EDGE Quad Band (850/900/1800/1900)
Connectivity	Bluetooth 2.1, USB 2.0
Physical size	97.8×49.5×11.2 mm
Weight	87 g
Form factor	Candybar

The **LG GD510**, also known as the **LG GD510 Pop (also called as Pep)** , is a touchscreen mobile phone made by LG Electronics. It was first announced on September 30, 2009 and was released in October 2009.

Features

- Touch Screen
- Java (MIDP 2.1)
- Music Player (MP3, AAC, AAC+, WMA)
- Music Multitasking (Messaging)
- Radio (Stereo FM Radio with RDS)
- Social Networking Integration (Facebook, Myspace, Twitter)
- Video Player (MPEG4, H.263, H.264)
- Optional Solar Panel for battery charging

Specifications

General

- Form Factor: Touchscreen
- Dimensions: 97.8 × 49.5 × 11.2 mm
- Weight: 87 g
- Main Screen Type: TFT touchscreen, 256K colors
- Main Screen Size/Resolution: 240 x 400 pixels, 3.0 inches
- Messaging: SMS, MMS, Email(With SSL)
- Operating System: Flash UI
- Built-in Handsfree: Yes
- Voice-dial/memo: Yes
- Vibration: Yes
- Organiser: Yes
- Battery Stand-By: Up to 360 h
- Battery Talk Time: Up to 3 h 20 m

Connectivity

- 2G Network: GSM 850 / 900 / 1800 / 1900
- Bluetooth: Yes, v2.1 with A2DP
- USB: Yes, microUSB fh

Multimedia

- 3.15MP camera: 3.15 MP, 2048x1536 pixels, video(QVGA 15fps)
- Internal Memory: 42 MB shared memory
- Memory Slot: microSD, up to 16GB
- Games: Yes
- Music: MP3 player
- Radio: Yes
- Ringtones: Polyphonic, MP3
- Speakers: Built-in handsfree speakerphone

References

External Links

Lg Pop Forum [1]

GU230

GU230

The "GU230" is a mobile phone manufactured by LG Electronics. The phone is designed to be low cost, and provide the essentials.

Manufacturer	LG Electronics
Carrier	Crazy John's
Available	Q4 2009
Screen	2.2"
Camera	Yes
Operating system	S-Class
Input	Keypad
Networks	GSM 850/900/1800/1900, GPRS Class 12, EDGE Class 12
Connectivity	Bluetooth
Battery	3.7V 900mAh
Physical size	104 x 48 x 15.2 mm
Weight	89g
Form factor	Slider

Main Features

The LG GU230 is a basic slider phone. The key features are:

- Tactile keypad
- 2.2" LCD Screen
- FM Player (with recording)
- 1.3 Megapixel camera
- WAP
- Speaker Phone (Handsfree)
- CLDC 1.1 and MIDP 2.0 Java Support
- In-built Games
- 3D S-Class User Interface

- Calendar and Organiser
- Alarm
- Customisable Wallpaper
- Downloadable Ringtones & Wallpapers

In The Box

When you buy the phone you should get:

- LG GU230 Mobile Phone
- LG Approved GU230 900mAh 3.7V Li-Ion Battery
- A/C Charger
- Handsfree (Headset with Microphone)

Technical Specifications

Here are the technical specifications of this phone.

Carrier Support

Theoretically, the phone should work on any network, if you unlock it. However, according to the phones website [1], the phone will work on Crazy Johns only.

Operating Frequency

GSM: 850/900/1500/1900
UMTS: GPRS Class 12/EDGE Class 12

Dimensions

Height: 104mm
Width: 48mm
Thickness: 15.2mm
Weight: 89g

Screen

Size:2.2" LCD
Colours: 262k
Pixels:176x200 (Width x Height)

Memory

Internal: 6 Megabytes
Expandable: Yes, up to 2 Gigabytes MicroSD **Phone Book:** Up to 1000 Entries

Messaging

The phone can send normal SMS text messages (with T9 (predictive text), as well as MMS, with Video MMS capabilities. The phone also has email capabilities.

Camera

The phone has a 1.3 MegaPixel camera with 2 times digital zoom.

Media

Music: Audio formats include MP3, AAC, WMA, RA, AMR and MIDI
Video: Video formats include H.263, and MPEG4
The phone also comes with a FM Radio, and like most other phones you need the headset that comes with the phone.

Battery

The battery that comes with the phone is 3.7V 900mAh Li-Ion, with 350 hours of stand-by time and 3.5 hours of talk time.

Connectivity

The phone comes with Bluetooth and a can be synced with a PC, but you have to buy the USB cable separately. It has a web upload speed of 48kbps

See also

LG Electronics
LG Electronics Australia [2]

LG Chocolate (VX8575)

LG Chocolate (VX8575)

Manufacturer	LG
Camera	3.2 Megapixel
Networks	Verizon Wireless

The **LG VX8575**, often times referred to simply as the **LG Chocolate Touch**, is the fourth cellular phone in the popular LG Chocolate line with the Verizon Wireless network. Like the other Chocolate phones, the phone has an MP3 player that runs on Dolby Mobile. Since its release in November 2009, roughly 1.2 million devices have been sold. Also the LG Chocolate Touch has an 3.2 megapixel camera.

External links

- LG Chocolate Touch Official Page [1]
- LG Chocolate Touch Fans Group [2]

LG GT365

LG GT365

The **LG Neon** is a semi-touchscreen phone that only uses the touchscreen as a dialer and looking up people on your contacts list. This phone is an entry-level device that cuts out many features, such as 3G and Wi-Fi. This device does have a 2 megapixel camera, full QWERTY keyboard, and Bluetooth that can be used to transfer files between other devices. This cellular phone also has a micro SD card slot that can support up to 4 GB of memory.

LG LU2300

LG LU2300

Manufacturer	LG Electronics
Screen	800 x 480 px
Camera	5 megapixel autofocus with LED flash
Operating system	Android 2.1 (upgradable to 2.2)
Input	Multi-touch capacitive touchscreen display, QWERTY keyboard, Touch-sensitive optical trackpad
CPU	Qualcomm Snapdragon QSD8250, 1 GHz
Memory	512 MiB RAM, 512 MiB ROM
Connectivity	GSM850/900/1800/1900, HSDPA, 802.11b/g/n
Related	LG Optimus

The **LG LU2300**, also known as the **LG Optimus Q** is a high-end smartphone manufactured by LG Electronics for the South Korean market. It is LG's first high-end handset to run Google's Android operating system.

The handset features a slide-out QWERTY keyboard, and a capacitive touchscreen display.

See also

- List of Android devices

LG VS740

LG VS740

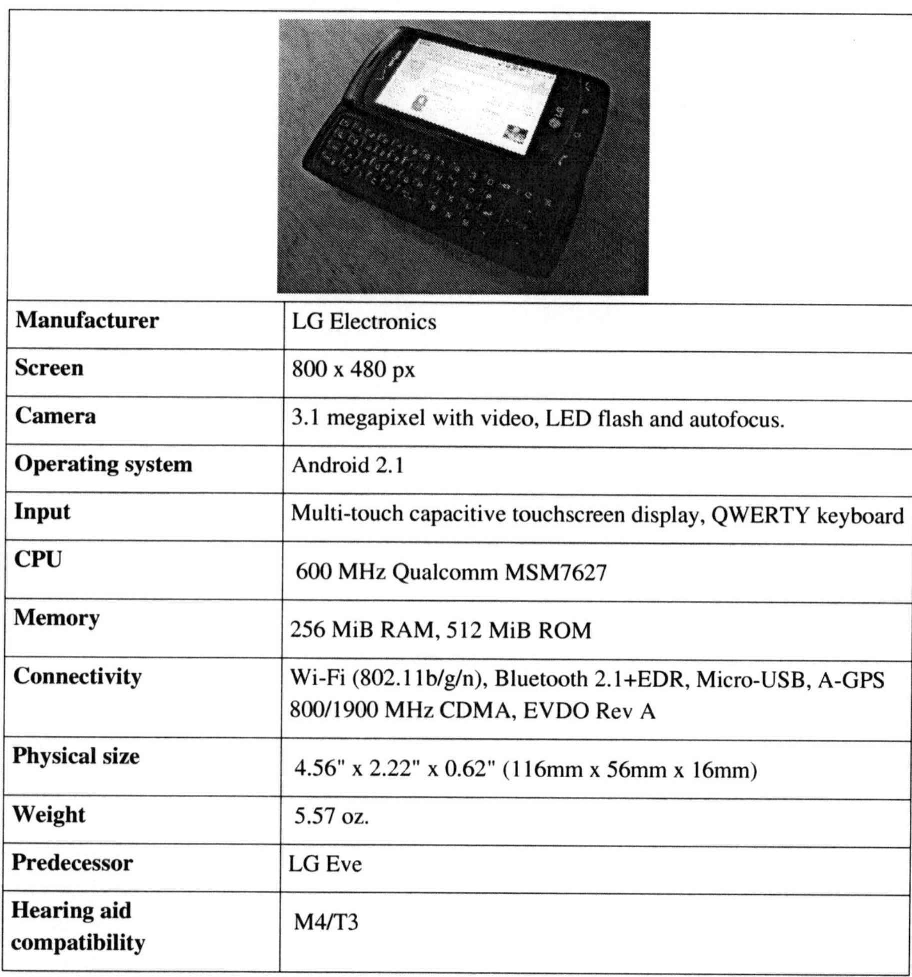

Manufacturer	LG Electronics
Screen	800 x 480 px
Camera	3.1 megapixel with video, LED flash and autofocus.
Operating system	Android 2.1
Input	Multi-touch capacitive touchscreen display, QWERTY keyboard
CPU	600 MHz Qualcomm MSM7627
Memory	256 MiB RAM, 512 MiB ROM
Connectivity	Wi-Fi (802.11b/g/n), Bluetooth 2.1+EDR, Micro-USB, A-GPS 800/1900 MHz CDMA, EVDO Rev A
Physical size	4.56" x 2.22" x 0.62" (116mm x 56mm x 16mm)
Weight	5.57 oz.
Predecessor	LG Eve
Hearing aid compatibility	M4/T3

The *LG Ally* (LG VS740) is a high-end smartphone manufactured by LG Electronics. It is LG's first Android-running device, and is exclusive to Verizon Wireless as a mid-range smartphone.

The Ally features a 3.2 inch, 800x480 LCD capacitive touchscreen display and a 3.2 megapixel camera with flash. It runs Android 2.1, with LG customizations, including a Themes application allowing the Ally to run LG's own launcher, similar to HTC Sense, Motoblur, and Touchwiz, although it is optional by default; and LG widgets including the Socialite application, which aggregates Facebook and Twitter. It also features a four-row slider keyboard with a d-pad.

It has a hearing-aid compatibility (HAC) rating of M4/T3

See also

- List of Android devices

LG GT540

LG GT540

Manufacturer	LG Electronics
Screen	3-inch 320 × 480 TFT resistive touchscreen
Camera	3 Megapixel autofocus
Operating system	Android 1.6 "Donut" (Update-able to Android 2.1)
CPU	Qualcomm MSM7227, 600 MHz
Memory	RAM: 256 MB, ROM: 256 MB
Memory card	up to 32 GB with microSDHC
Connectivity	GSM 850/900/1800/1900, UMTS 900/2100, HSDPA 7.2; Wi-Fi (802.11b/g); Bluetooth 2.1 + EDR; GPS with A-GPS; MicroUSB
Battery	Li-ion polymer 1500 mAh
Physical size	109 (4.3) × 54.5 (2.1) × 12.9 (0.5) mm (inch)
Weight	115.5 g (4.1 oz)
Form factor	Slate smartphone
Related	LG Optimus Q

The **LG Optimus (LG GT540)**, previously known as **LG GT540 Swift**, is a low-end smartphone manufactured by LG Electronics. The Optimus runs the 1.6 version of Android. It was designed for first time smartphone users which its slogan "Optimal performance for first time smartphone users" says. The phone provides four colours which are black, white, pink and silver. It was announced on April 27, 2010. It is now available worldwide. An official LG GT540 Android 2.1 (Eclair) update was released on 30th September 2010 for phones in the Baltic Region.. The update will be released in different regions throughout the rest of 2010. .

Reception

The LG GT540 received a generally positive reception.

TechRadar commented that: "Given that it's free on £15 a month contracts, you don't really have the right to expect top notch features. And, taking that into consideration, we have to say that the LG Optimus GT540 is a nicely rounded phone." Although the reviewer added that "there's nothing outstanding about it, but the features fit together well enough."

IT Reviews noted that the build quality was solid for a budget phone. The site said: "Build quality is reasonably good. The chassis is made from plastic which has been given a brushed metal finish."

Electricpig.co.uk was slightly less enthusiastic. While the reviewer praised the phone's "surprisingly pleasant media skills", they bemoaned the resistive screen, and preferred the older LG GW620 in some respects.

External links

- The LG Optimus (GT540) Official Website [1]
- LG Optimus on LGDroid.Net [2]

Article Sources and Contributors

LG Chocolate (VX8500) *Source*: http://en.wikipedia.org/?oldid=356830365 *Contributors*: Craig14

LG Chocolate (KG800) *Source*: http://en.wikipedia.org/?oldid=354374195 *Contributors*: Colonies Chris

LG VX8300 *Source*: http://en.wikipedia.org/?oldid=387826674 *Contributors*: Theleapist

LG The V (VX9800) *Source*: http://en.wikipedia.org/?oldid=343407326 *Contributors*: 1 anonymous edits

LG Prada (KE850) *Source*: http://en.wikipedia.org/?oldid=390127739 *Contributors*: Macserv

LG Chocolate (U830) *Source*: http://en.wikipedia.org/?oldid=342420547 *Contributors*: Tinton5

LG enV (VX9900) *Source*: http://en.wikipedia.org/?oldid=380403335 *Contributors*: 1 anonymous edits

LG Shine (KE970) *Source*: http://en.wikipedia.org/?oldid=390370871 *Contributors*: 1 anonymous edits

LG Aegis (MG320) *Source*: http://en.wikipedia.org/?oldid=354050168 *Contributors*: 1 anonymous edits

LG Black Zafiro (MG810) *Source*: http://en.wikipedia.org/?oldid=381667190 *Contributors*:

LG VX9400 *Source*: http://en.wikipedia.org/?oldid=331020412 *Contributors*:

LG CU500 *Source*: http://en.wikipedia.org/?oldid=354787863 *Contributors*: R'n'B

LG G 1500 *Source*: http://en.wikipedia.org/?oldid=295403129 *Contributors*: Kojozone

LG VX8700 *Source*: http://en.wikipedia.org/?oldid=342422883 *Contributors*: Tinton5

LG Shine (U970) *Source*: http://en.wikipedia.org/?oldid=376658073 *Contributors*: R'n'B

LG Viewty (KU990) *Source*: http://en.wikipedia.org/?oldid=387308302 *Contributors*:

LG Voyager (VX10000) *Source*: http://en.wikipedia.org/?oldid=368094109 *Contributors*: 1 anonymous edits

LG VX8800 *Source*: http://en.wikipedia.org/?oldid=382449914 *Contributors*: MER-C

LG VX8350 *Source*: http://en.wikipedia.org/?oldid=366760110 *Contributors*: 1 anonymous edits

PRADA (phone) *Source*: http://en.wikipedia.org/?oldid=357136636 *Contributors*:

LG Chocolate (TG800) *Source*: http://en.wikipedia.org/?oldid=363938241 *Contributors*: Tomtheeditor

LG Chocolate (KV5900) *Source*: http://en.wikipedia.org/?oldid=345186926 *Contributors*: Lorddragyn

List of LG mobile phones *Source*: http://en.wikipedia.org/?oldid=389465931 *Contributors*: 1 anonymous edits

LG Chocolate (VX8550) *Source*: http://en.wikipedia.org/?oldid=384823768 *Contributors*:

LG Chocolate Platinum (KE800) *Source*: http://en.wikipedia.org/?oldid=357174191 *Contributors*:

LG CU500v *Source*: http://en.wikipedia.org/?oldid=354788299 *Contributors*: R'n'B

LG Trax (CU575) *Source*: http://en.wikipedia.org/?oldid=354788504 *Contributors*: R'n'B

LG Secret (KF750) *Source*: http://en.wikipedia.org/?oldid=387308294 *Contributors*:

LG Black Label Series *Source*: http://en.wikipedia.org/?oldid=334167289 *Contributors*:

LG enV2 (VX9100) *Source*: http://en.wikipedia.org/?oldid=389355715 *Contributors*: Arbitrarily0

LG Rumor (LX260) *Source*: http://en.wikipedia.org/?oldid=390447060 *Contributors*: Woohookitty

LG Dare (VX9700) *Source*: http://en.wikipedia.org/?oldid=387987412 *Contributors*:

LG Vu (CU915/CU920) *Source*: http://en.wikipedia.org/?oldid=361164169 *Contributors*: Lester

LG KU 380 *Source*: http://en.wikipedia.org/?oldid=345187550 *Contributors*: Lorddragyn

LG Chocolate (VX8560) *Source*: http://en.wikipedia.org/?oldid=371015621 *Contributors*: 1 anonymous edits

LG VX8100 *Source*: http://en.wikipedia.org/?oldid=386756630 *Contributors*:

LG KS20 *Source*: http://en.wikipedia.org/?oldid=381070056 *Contributors*: ZirconiumTwice

LG Renoir (KC910) *Source*: http://en.wikipedia.org/?oldid=388782552 *Contributors*: Logan

LG Cookie (KP500) *Source*: http://en.wikipedia.org/?oldid=387517775 *Contributors*: Ajinkya22

LG KS360 *Source*: http://en.wikipedia.org/?oldid=378271251 *Contributors*: Mahewa

LG GD910 *Source*: http://en.wikipedia.org/?oldid=376073441 *Contributors*: 1 anonymous edits

LG GD900 *Source*: http://en.wikipedia.org/?oldid=373539307 *Contributors*: Feudonym

LG KM900 (Arena) *Source*: http://en.wikipedia.org/?oldid=387308288 *Contributors*:

KF510 *Source*: http://en.wikipedia.org/?oldid=378568883 *Contributors*: R'n'B

LG CT810 Incite *Source*: http://en.wikipedia.org/?oldid=387538628 *Contributors*: 1 anonymous edits

LG KF600 *Source*: http://en.wikipedia.org/?oldid=342418179 *Contributors*: Tinton5

LG KG290 *Source*: http://en.wikipedia.org/?oldid=328210506 *Contributors*: Gilly of III

LG enV Touch (VX11000) *Source*: http://en.wikipedia.org/?oldid=383750428 *Contributors*: 1 anonymous edits

LG Rumor 2 *Source*: http://en.wikipedia.org/?oldid=388776676 *Contributors*: Logan

LG Lotus (LX600) *Source*: http://en.wikipedia.org/?oldid=389717583 *Contributors*: Cobollam

LG Xenon *Source*: http://en.wikipedia.org/?oldid=390096689 *Contributors*: Philip Trueman

LG enV3 (VX9200) *Source*: http://en.wikipedia.org/?oldid=390425195 *Contributors*: 1 anonymous edits

LG Prada II (KF900) *Source*: http://en.wikipedia.org/?oldid=388391098 *Contributors*: Bsadowski1

LG Viewty Smart *Source*: http://en.wikipedia.org/?oldid=387980660 *Contributors*: LilHelpa

LG Versa *Source*: http://en.wikipedia.org/?oldid=362908074 *Contributors*: 1 anonymous edits

GW525 *Source*: http://en.wikipedia.org/?oldid=370966579 *Contributors*:

LG Chocolate (BL40) *Source*: http://en.wikipedia.org/?oldid=387308278 *Contributors*:

LG VX5500 *Source*: http://en.wikipedia.org/?oldid=363063703 *Contributors*: Alex.szatmary

LG GW620 *Source*: http://en.wikipedia.org/?oldid=385378977 *Contributors*: Nomader

Vx8360 *Source*: http://en.wikipedia.org/?oldid=360541146 *Contributors*: Malcolma

LG eXpo *Source*: http://en.wikipedia.org/?oldid=381064852 *Contributors*: ZirconiumTwice

LG CF360 *Source*: http://en.wikipedia.org/?oldid=381812035 *Contributors*: Dwayne

LG GD510 *Source*: http://en.wikipedia.org/?oldid=388477452 *Contributors*: 1 anonymous edits

GU230 *Source*: http://en.wikipedia.org/?oldid=370965289 *Contributors*:

LG Chocolate (VX8575) *Source*: http://en.wikipedia.org/?oldid=387322590 *Contributors*: 1 anonymous edits

LG GT365 *Source*: http://en.wikipedia.org/?oldid=365735156 *Contributors*: 1 anonymous edits

LG LU2300 *Source*: http://en.wikipedia.org/?oldid=390254191 *Contributors*: Woohookitty

LG VS740 *Source*: http://en.wikipedia.org/?oldid=390254186 *Contributors*: Woohookitty

LG GT540 *Source*: http://en.wikipedia.org/?oldid=389147299 *Contributors*: 1 anonymous edits

Image Sources, Licenses and Contributors

Image:LG Chocolate Phone Open.jpg *Source*: http://en.wikipedia.org/w/index.php?title=File:LG_Chocolate_Phone_Open.jpg *License*: Public Domain *Contributors*: User:The Random Editor

File:Flag of the United States.svg *Source*: http://en.wikipedia.org/w/index.php?title=File:Flag_of_the_United_States.svg *License*: Public Domain *Contributors*: User:Dbenbenn, User:Indolences, User:Jacobolus, User:Technion, User:Zscout370

File:Flag of Canada.svg *Source*: http://en.wikipedia.org/w/index.php?title=File:Flag_of_Canada.svg *License*: Public Domain *Contributors*: User:E Pluribus Anthony, User:Mzajac

Image:LG Viewty.jpg *Source*: http://en.wikipedia.org/w/index.php?title=File:LG_Viewty.jpg *License*: Creative Commons Attribution 2.0 *Contributors*: sylvainratton

Image:LG Voyager VX10000 External .jpg *Source*: http://en.wikipedia.org/w/index.php?title=File:LG_Voyager_VX10000_External_.jpg *License*: Public Domain *Contributors*: User:ZeWrestler

Image:LG Voyager VX10000 Internal.jpg *Source*: http://en.wikipedia.org/w/index.php?title=File:LG_Voyager_VX10000_Internal.jpg *License*: Public Domain *Contributors*: User:ZeWrestler

File:Flag of South Korea.svg *Source*: http://en.wikipedia.org/w/index.php?title=File:Flag_of_South_Korea.svg *License*: Public Domain *Contributors*: Various

Image:Image-LGChocolateVX8550Red.jpeg *Source*: http://en.wikipedia.org/w/index.php?title=File:Image-LGChocolateVX8550Red.jpeg *License*: Public Domain *Contributors*: Original uploader was DivineBaboon at en.wikipedia

Image:LG enV2 (VX9100).JPG *Source*: http://en.wikipedia.org/w/index.php?title=File:LG_enV2_(VX9100).JPG *License*: Creative Commons Attribution-Sharealike 3.0 *Contributors*: User:Arbitrarily0

Image:LG LX260, front - closed.jpg *Source*: http://en.wikipedia.org/w/index.php?title=File:LG_LX260,_front_-_closed.jpg *License*: Creative Commons Attribution-Sharealike 3.0 *Contributors*: User:Editor at Large

File:LG LX260, front - open.jpg *Source*: http://en.wikipedia.org/w/index.php?title=File:LG_LX260,_front_-_open.jpg *License*: Creative Commons Attribution-Sharealike 3.0 *Contributors*: User:Editor at Large

File:LG LX260, back - closed.jpg *Source*: http://en.wikipedia.org/w/index.php?title=File:LG_LX260,_back_-_closed.jpg *License*: Creative Commons Attribution-Sharealike 3.0 *Contributors*: User:Editor at Large

Image:Lgvx8560a.JPG *Source*: http://en.wikipedia.org/w/index.php?title=File:Lgvx8560a.JPG *License*: Public Domain *Contributors*: Lex

Image:Lgvx8560b.JPG *Source*: http://en.wikipedia.org/w/index.php?title=File:Lgvx8560b.JPG *License*: Public Domain *Contributors*: Lex

Image:LG Renoir (LG-KC910) (3286620784).jpg *Source*: http://en.wikipedia.org/w/index.php?title=File:LG_Renoir_(LG-KC910)_(3286620784).jpg *License*: Creative Commons Attribution 2.0 *Contributors*: LGEPR

Image:Lgkp570.JPG *Source*: http://en.wikipedia.org/w/index.php?title=File:Lgkp570.JPG *License*: Creative Commons Attribution 2.0 *Contributors*: edusand

Image:Lg-ks360-fan.JPG *Source*: http://en.wikipedia.org/w/index.php?title=File:Lg-ks360-fan.JPG *License*: Public Domain *Contributors*: User:LorDDeviL

Image:Lg gd900 phone 1.jpg *Source*: http://en.wikipedia.org/w/index.php?title=File:Lg_gd900_phone_1.jpg *License*: Creative Commons Attribution-Sharealike 3.0 *Contributors*: User:Jontintinjordan

Image:LG Arena.jpg *Source*: http://en.wikipedia.org/w/index.php?title=File:LG_Arena.jpg *License*: Creative Commons Attribution-Sharealike 3.0 *Contributors*: User:Jontintinjordan

File:Telefonecelular.jpg *Source*: http://en.wikipedia.org/w/index.php?title=File:Telefonecelular.jpg *License*: Creative Commons Attribution-Sharealike 3.0 *Contributors*: User:EUDOXIO

Image:2 (RUMOR) (3670122420).jpg *Source*: http://en.wikipedia.org/w/index.php?title=File:2_(RUMOR)_(3670122420).jpg *License*: Creative Commons Attribution 2.0 *Contributors*: LGEPR

Image:LG EnV3.jpg *Source*: http://en.wikipedia.org/w/index.php?title=File:LG_EnV3.jpg *License*: Creative Commons Attribution 3.0 *Contributors*: User:Jpferdehirt

File:LG-GW525, GW520 Orange (3626911515).jpg *Source*: http://en.wikipedia.org/w/index.php?title=File:LG-GW525,_GW520_Orange_(3626911515).jpg *License*: Creative Commons Attribution 2.0 *Contributors*: LGEPR

Image:LGAlly.JPG *Source*: http://en.wikipedia.org/w/index.php?title=File:LGAlly.JPG *License*: Public Domain *Contributors*: Wikipedia:en:User:IndiemonIndiemon

CPSIA information can be obtained at www.ICGtesting.com
Printed in the USA
LVOW051803291112
309390LV00006B/493/P